Wheels

"I always wanted to be a writer, but growing up in a working class family background in the west of Scotland, with a widowed mother and three sisters, being a writer was a dream I thought could never come true. It was only after my youngest child was born that I started sending stories away.

I wrote every kind of story, from horror to romance, but began to realise I had a knack for writing comedy. I thought I'd found the kind of writing I wanted to do until my daughter Katie was bullied in school and I wrote my first children's book, *Run Zak Run*. Now I love writing for children too."

Catherine MacPhail

Wheels

CATHERINE MACPHAIL

Heinemann

Inspiring generations

Heinemann Educational Publishers
Halley Court, Jordan Hill, Oxford OX2 8EJ
Part of Harcourt Education

Heinemann is the registered trademark of
Harcourt Education Limited

First published in Great Britain in 2003 by the Penguin Group
First published in the New Windmills Series in 2005

5

British Library Cataloguing in Publication Data is available
from the British Library on request.

10-digit ISBN: 0 435131 05 2
13-digit ISBN: 978 0 435131 05 0

Cover photo: Getty Images/Imageback
Cover design by Words and Publications
Typeset by 🪾 Tek-Art, Croydon, Surrey

Printed in China by CTPS

To my friend Sandra, who always listens

The author would like to thank Gordon Murray for his help.

Chapter 1

The rain was blinding me and the wipers were working frantically to try to clear the windscreen.

Dad called back to me. 'All right, James?' He smiled. 'Soon be home.'

Sitting in the back seat, I could already see familiar landmarks and junctions. Dad nodded across to where Mum sat, sound asleep. 'So much for her staying awake and doing the navigating.'

Mum had promised solemnly that she would. She didn't want to drive, she said. I knew she'd been glad that Dad hadn't pressed her to take the wheel. So was I, to be honest. Mum's driving was erratic to say the least. And she always managed to miss a turn-off. All I wanted now, after our holiday, was home.

She wasn't the only one who wanted to doze. I could hardly keep my eyes open, but I wouldn't let myself sleep for Dad's sake. Dad was tired too. Must be – he'd been driving all day, all the way from down south. I knew that it was only my chatter that would be keeping him awake.

'It was a great holiday, wasn't it, Dad?'

The best yet,' Dad said. 'But next year I'll beat you in the father–son race. You wait and see.'

'You wish,' I laughed. 'You're getting past it, Dad. You'll be using a zimmer by next year.'

'If I wasn't driving this car, boy, I'd clip you round the ear.'

I shouted. 'Stop this car now! I'm going to phone Childline!'

Dad started to sing then. Some old song about being 'just a poor boy from a poor family'. I would have joined in if I'd know what the heck the song was.

1

'When we get home I'll make some mince and potatoes, *mi amigo*!'

'Aye, aye, aye! Big man.' Mince and mashed potatoes. Dad's speciality. I'd never tasted anything quite like my dad's mince and mash, and it had become a custom that he always made it when we came back from holiday.

'I'll put in my special ingredient,' he told me. 'My toenail clippings!'

'Ah, so that's what the crunchy bits are!'

And Dad began singing again.

Far off in the distance, headlights shimmered towards us. Too bright, I thought. Why didn't people think to put the dimmer switch on?

'We turn off at the next junction, Dad.'

'We do, *mi amigo*. You're a better navigator than your mother.'

'That's not a compliment,' I said. 'Anyone's a better navigator than she is.'

I watched as those headlights seemed to rush towards us. It must be this rain, I was thinking, because it looked like the white van was veering over to our side of the road. But when I glanced at Dad, he didn't seem too worried. It must be my imagination, I decided.

Home soon, I was thinking, and my own bed, and mince and potatoes. And tomorrow Dad was taking me to the big match.

Life, I decided, didn't get much better than this.

'You're a great son, James. Did I ever tell you that?' Dad said suddenly. Never one to dish out compliments, this one took me by surprise.

'Are you trying to borrow money or something?'

Dad was rubbing the tiredness away from his eyes. 'There's something I want you to remember...' he began, but he didn't finish for in that second he yelled, '*MY GOD!*' I leaned forward. The van *was* shooting towards us, on our side of the road!

I was trying to see the driver, but the rain . . . the lights were blinding me. Dad was struggling with the wheel, trying desperately to avoid the van that was skidding right at us.

'*DAD!*' I screamed. I glanced at him, saw the panic on his face. Panic? On my dad's face! What was happening?

Chaos!

Terror!

The van still hurtling in our direction. Everything happening too quickly.

Blinding lights. The world upside down.

Yells.

Flashes.

Screams.

'Dad!' I was shouting. '*DAAADDD!*'

'Are you all right, James?' My mother was shaking me awake as she drew the car to a halt. 'Bad dream?' She turned off the ignition, not waiting for my answer. 'We're here,' she said, and she got out of the car and opened the boot.

I could feel tears sting at my eyes as I blearily opened them. It had been a dream. A nightmare. The worst nightmare of my life. My mother was opening my door, holding something in her hand. Her face was worried.

'Sure you're all right?'

I barely nodded, still caught up in the nightmare. Still trying to shake it off.

She smiled. 'Good,' she said.

And then she moved and I saw what she was holding.

A wheelchair.

My wheelchair.

It hadn't been a nightmare. It had been a memory. It had really happened. The crash. My dad, gone forever. Me in a wheelchair.

And we weren't at home.

We were at the hospital.

And, inside, I screamed again.

Chapter 2

'You had the dream again, didn't you?' my mother asked as she wheeled me inside the hospital.

'I wouldn't call it a dream. It's a nightmare.'

She touched my shoulder and I shrank from her. 'I know how you feel, James,' she said.

'No, you don't!' My answer was sharp. She didn't. She'd slept through it all. Maybe if she hadn't . . .

Always the same thought, especially after the nightmare. If she hadn't, Dad would have been more aware of the van skidding towards us. Dad might still be here. I might still be able to walk.

'Anyway, big day today,' she carried on with a false cheeriness. She could be cheery really. She was alive. She could walk. A miraculous escape, the doctors had said. Lucky old Mum.

'Maybe today,' she went on, 'we'll get some good news.'

Good news? More operations, more tests. But I'd never be able to walk again, and being able to walk again was the only good news I wanted.

Now – after the nightmare – I felt as if I'd just lost my dad all over again. I could still hear him singing, 'I'm just a poor boy from a poor family.'

Dad!

'Hello, James.' I knew the nurse who stopped to talk to us. I looked up at her. 'Good to see you again,' she said, smiling. She was nice, always tried to be friendly. I wouldn't smile back. I hated having to look up at people. I hated this wheelchair.

I turned away from her and she continued to talk to my mother. It was as if I wasn't there, as if I had suddenly become invisible.

'I hope he gets good news, Mrs Gordon,' she said.

I didn't hear my mother's reply. But I knew by the silence that she must be mouthing something to her, something she didn't want me to hear.

Did they think I'd disappeared? Why didn't they talk to *me*? Did they think my ears didn't work either?

Mum wheeled me into a waiting room crowded with people. No one glanced my way. I WAS invisible. I preferred it that way. When I was noticed, it was usually with a sympathetic smile. Who needed that?

'I'll just leave you here, dear.' My mother crouched beside me. 'I'll go and let them know we've arrived.' She smiled, hoping for me to smile back. I didn't. I couldn't. I could hardly bring myself to look at her.

'I'm not going anywhere,' I snapped. 'I can't exactly run away.'

Her cheeks flushed and she stood up. 'I'll only be a minute.'

I watched her as she walked to the receptionist's desk. 'She's got a good pair of legs on her, my mother,' I used to tell Dad. And Dad would laugh and reply, 'I've seen better ones on a table.'

'I'm outnumbered here,' she would say. 'Two to one.'

She wasn't outnumbered any more. One of the two had gone. Forever.

I looked round the waiting room without interest. I didn't care what anyone else was here for. The woman whose lips trembled as she clutched nervously at her handbag. The girl, just about my age, who sat squeezing her mother's hand. The girl's eyes were filled: on the edge of tears. Who cared what their problems were? I had my own. People came and went through the swing doors. Nurses, orderlies, patients. Paramedics hurrying to their next case.

My mother had disappeared, probably in search of the consultant who'd been dealing with my case. Mr Thomas.

I wondered what he would have to tell her. Had he found a miracle cure? I would walk again? It was what I wanted All I wanted. To be out of this wheelchair, to stand up again. To walk. To run. Sometimes I wished I'd died with my father. Anything was better than life in this thing.

Yet I knew deep down it could never happen.

My attention was caught as the swing doors were pushed open again and a bustling crowd came through. Two laughing nurses, a little man in a white coat who looked more like a painter and decorator than a doctor, and someone else. A young man, early twenties maybe, but I couldn't make out his face, walking as he was behind the rest.

But there was something about the shape of his head, his floppy fair hair, that made me keep watching him as he strode down the corridors towards the exit doors.

Where had I seen him before? I began to wheel myself to the entrance for a better view. The man was young, slim, taking long strides towards the door.

Had I perhaps seen him here, in the hospital, on one of my many visits? I didn't think so.

And yet there was something so familiar about him.

I found I was wheeling after him. If I could just see his face. But the man didn't turn as he headed for the door.

Had I seen him on television? Now there was an idea. Perhaps he was in one of the many hospital programmes that were always on TV. But no, I avoided watching those like the plague nowadays.

I began to wheel faster, aware that at any moment the man would reach the exit doors, pass through them, be gone forever.

And I *had* to know who he was. Why was it so important? I couldn't explain it. I hurried after him, brushing against impatient people in my path.

Then, just as the man reached the exit, he looked back. Just for a second. As if he knew someone was following

6

him. As if he was aware of my eyes boring into his back, willing him to turn.

He fastened his bright blue eyes on mine.

I caught my breath. Beads of cold, icy sweat began to trickle down my back. I was in my nightmare again. Heard the yells and screams, the lights flashing, the world turning upside down.

Now I recognised the face I had never been able to make out before. I was staring into the eyes of the man who had been driving the vehicle that had killed my dad.

Chapter 3

And, suddenly, he was gone.

The man who had ruined my life had disappeared. I couldn't let that happen. Frantically, I wheeled myself towards the doors, not caring who I was ramming into.

'Move!' I screamed at a young pregnant woman crossing my path. She glared at me. They all did. I was like a juggernaut, letting nothing stand in my way. They jumped aside, muttering in indignation.

At the doors, I stopped. I couldn't get through. This was not the automatic exit I had come through with my mother. These were the swing doors further down the corridor, not wheelchair accessible, and I couldn't get through them. I yelled aloud with frustration and banged against them with the wheelchair.

'Do you want me to open them for you, dear?' an old lady asked.

'I'm not your dear! And yes, open the door!'

She flushed with embarrassment. 'Sorry,' she said.

I was making a scene and I knew it. I was almost in tears with frustrated anger. But I had to get through.

'Shouldn't he be with someone?' The stupid old bat aimed her question at the gathering crowd.

That was the last straw. 'You can talk to me!' I screamed. 'And I don't have to be with anyone. I'm in a wheelchair. I'm not from another planet.'

'I'd send you to another planet if you were my son,' a man snapped at me.

'Well, I'm not. So open this door!'

The man sneered at me. 'Open it yourself if you're that clever.'

I wanted to jump on him. Leap from the chair and wrestle him to the ground. They were all staring at me now. Some with disgust. Most with pity.

I preferred the disgust any day.

'James? What's wrong?' My mother, rushing towards me, concerned, embarrassed. Apologising for me. I hated her for that. 'James, what's going on?'

She moved me to a corner, in spite of my protests. She had to understand how vital it was for us to leave this hospital *now*! Nothing else mattered.

'We've got to follow him. He's getting away.'

'Follow who? Who's getting away?'

She was beside me, looking into my eyes.

I grabbed her hand. Her eyes flashed, surprised at the contact. I touched her so seldom. 'I saw him. He was here, in the hospital. And now, if we don't hurry, he's going to get away.'

She smiled patiently. 'Just who are you talking about, James?'

I took a deep breath. 'The man who was driving the van that night. The man who killed Dad.'

I expected shock. I even expected tears. I didn't expect her to flush, get to her feet and calmly begin pushing me back to the waiting room again.

I wanted so much to get to my feet, drag her out of the hospital. Confront her. Instead, I shouted at the top of my voice so everyone stopped and turned to look at us. 'Did you hear me? I saw the man who killed Dad!'

My mother gasped and suddenly she was on her knees in front of me.

'No, you didn't, James.' She said it softly. Yet it sounded almost like a scream.

'I did, I tell you. I did. I know I've always said I can't remember his face. It's always been a blur, too many lights; even in the nightmare I can't remember. But just now . . . honest, Mum. You have to believe me.' This time

9

I squeezed her hand tightly. 'I saw him. He was in this hospital and he walked out of that door.'

She was shaking her head. 'You were mistaken. It wasn't him.'

Now I was angry again. I threw her hand from me. 'How would you know? You slept through it all.'

If that hurt, she hid it. Perhaps I had said it so often it didn't bother her any more. She stood up.

'Mr Thomas is waiting for us.'

'To hell with Mr Thomas!' I yelled.

A couple of nurses looked at me angrily, as if they'd like to take the brake off my wheelchair on a steep hill.

'We have to go to the police. Tell them.' I looked up at my mother. 'This is important information.' It was almost a plea. I was nearly begging her.

She touched my face gently. 'I'm sorry, James. I don't know who you saw, but it wasn't the man who was driving the van that night. It couldn't have been.'

For a moment I said nothing. Just looked at her, puzzled. Finally I asked, 'Why couldn't it have been?'

It seemed to me that my mother took a long time to answer. 'Because the driver of the van was killed that night too.'

Chapter 4

My mother wheeled me on as if nothing had happened. As if it would all be forgotten.

Forgotten?

My heart was thumping in my chest. I wanted to yell out to her, but I couldn't find my voice.

The driver was DEAD? But the man I'd seen wasn't dead, was he?

Was he?

I remembered Dad once telling me a ghost story, and in it the spirits were as real and solid as everyone else. No one knew they were dead.

'We see ghosts all the time,' Dad had said, eerily. 'And we don't even know it. They pass us on the street, sit beside us on buses, haunt places they used to go to when they were alive.'

Had I seen a ghost?

No! Dad had told me it was only a story, just a story. Not a word of truth in it. I didn't believe in ghosts.

But I couldn't get it out of my head.

I tugged at Mum's hand. 'He definitely died? The other driver?'

She leaned down to me. 'We didn't tell you anything about it. You were so ill in hospital. He was just a teenager. His family was as devastated as we were by the accident.

That made me angry. 'He caused it. At least he deserved to die.' I snapped out the words without thinking, but I meant them just the same.

'James, he was only a boy. He didn't mean for it to happen.'

But I could still picture him, on the wrong side of the road, heading straight for us. 'He caused it,' I said coldly. 'And I'm glad he's dead.'

My mother let out an anguished sigh. She didn't say anything but I knew what she was thinking: Don't be so bitter, James.

Well, I *was* bitter. I'd lost my life too in that accident. I couldn't walk. I'd never walk again.

Mr Thomas, the consultant, examined me thoroughly. He studied case notes and X-rays, sucking on his teeth, his glasses perched on top of his head. I kept thinking, Why doesn't he ever wear them? Are they just for effect? Doesn't he need them? My mind was in a whirl, hardly listening to the doctor's words. One face kept floating into my thoughts.

A ghost?

I couldn't believe that. I wouldn't believe that. Yet, if he wasn't a ghost . . . how could I have seen him?

Mr Thomas sat back in his chair, took the glasses from his head and swivelled them round his fingers. 'I'll arrange for you to come into the hospital, James. Not for a couple of months, but I want to do more tests.'

My mother grinned like an idiot and Mr Thomas shook his head at her. 'Don't get too excited, Mrs Gordon. These are only tests. We can't promise any real improvement. But we'll keep trying.'

More tests, I thought. Painful tests. And for what? More disappointment.

My mother drove home in silence, glancing my way now and then, anxiety written all over her face. 'Are you OK, James? I'm sorry it wasn't better news.'

But I hadn't even been thinking about Mr Thomas or his tests. All I could think of was the young man I had seen at the hospital. 'He *was* the driver, Mum,' I blurted out. 'I wasn't mistaken.'

'It couldn't have been him. It was just someone who looked like him. Who reminded you of him. Seeing someone similar just brought it all back.'

I tried to tell her that was rubbish, but she wouldn't listen. 'Don't think about it any more,' she insisted. 'I'll make us something nice for tea.' She smiled at me. 'Mince and potatoes. Mmm, you love mince and potatoes.'

'You don't make it like Dad used to,' I wanted to say, but I couldn't. It would have been too cruel, and it would have hurt me almost as much as it would have hurt her.

So we ate the mince and potatoes in silence. We did so much in silence these days, Mum and I. Hardly ever speaking. She always tried to be so nice to me, but I hated that. Hated being dependent on her, and she knew it.

She'd given up everything to look after me, never went anywhere without me. She'd resigned from her teaching job, so she could give me lessons at home. And, instead of being grateful, I resented it, and couldn't help myself.

I lay in bed that night going over the events of the day. I saw again the young man turning his face towards me, saw again those blue, blue eyes. And I could see him again so clearly at the wheel of that van as it hurtled at us. Those eyes, wild and frightened, caught in the headlights of our car.

It *had* been him I had seen at the hospital. Not someone who looked like him. Him!

But the driver had died.

I don't believe in ghosts, I kept telling myself. But I couldn't explain it any other way.

If only I wasn't so useless. If only I could have run after him, confronted him. I would have the answer right now.

But I was in a wheelchair. Helpless. I'd never know the answer.

I fell asleep, angry and full of despair.

Yet it was amazing what a good night's sleep could do, because I woke up in the morning with my next move clear in my head.

13

I'd never seen any newspaper reports of the accident. I'd been too ill in hospital, and my mother had kept any news from me – to protect me, I suppose.

But I would see those reports now. I couldn't do much from a wheelchair, but I could do this. I'd go to the library. The small local one near our house had a reading room and newspapers that went back for years.

Yes, I was going to the library, and I was going to read everything I could about the crash. I was going to find out the truth about the driver of the other vehicle.

Chapter 5

It had been a long time since I'd had the motivation to do anything. I sat around, I lay on my bed, I watched television. Depressed. Alone – because I shunned my friends now. Ash and Paul had been my two best friends all through school, from primary right into my first year at secondary. We had been a team once, the three of us, but not now. They could still walk and run and play football. Now, no matter how often they phoned or called at the house, I never wanted to see them or to talk to them. They were part of my past, a past that reminded me too much of how things used to be.

My mother's constantly worried frown annoyed me too. I hated the way she was always watching me.

So I wasn't surprised when I wheeled into the living room that morning, ready to go out, to see that frown turn to amazement.

'You want to go somewhere?' She beamed with surprised pleasure. 'I'll get my coat. Where do you want to go?'

Already she was pulling out the plug of the vacuum cleaner, stepping out of her slippers.

The last thing I needed was my mother coming with me. 'I'm just going to the library. I want to go on my own.'

She looked alarmed at that prospect. 'On your own . . . but, James . . .'

I tried not to be annoyed. Tried to tell myself she was only concerned about me. 'I've got to start going out by myself. The library's two corners away. All flat. And you can see it from the window. It won't be a problem.'

She didn't want me to go alone. Tried everything to persuade me that we should go together. Finally,

I couldn't help it: I lost my temper. 'I'm nearly thirteen. I'm too old to have my mum tag along everywhere with me, wheelchair or not. And if you don't let me try this on my own, I'll never leave this house again. OK?'

Yet, as I wheeled myself along our quiet street, I was apprehensive. What if I met up with a crowd of yobs and they pushed me over? What if the wheels of the chair got stuck in a crack and I couldn't move? I'd feel such a fool.

At the first corner I very nearly turned back. As I waited to cross the street all sorts of nightmares crowded into my mind. What if . . . halfway across, a car suddenly veered round the corner and hurled me and my chair into the air?

I had never felt so vulnerable in my life.

'You OK, James? Want a hand across the road?'

One of our neighbours, Mr Willoughby, peeked over his hedge.

I shook my head and, anxious to be away from his help, I took my chance and crossed the road without thinking. I didn't want anyone helping me. I'd manage fine.

And I did. By the time I'd reached the library some of my old confidence had returned.

Until I saw the stairs, that is.

The library was housed in an old Victorian building, with a set of ten stairs leading to the main entrance.

Stairs!

It might as well have been Mount Everest. It was the same challenge to me.

Where was the ramp? Where was the entrance for the disabled?

I felt the anger build up in me. Why did everything have to be so difficult?

Just then, the bespectacled librarian appeared at the top of the stairs.

'Can I help you up here?' she asked cheerily.

'This is ridiculous!' I snapped at her. 'This is against the law. There should be a ramp.'

She trotted down the stairs, agreeing with me. 'Tell me about it. They can't decide whether to build a ramp or just knock the place down. This council couldn't run a bus. Honestly.' She laughed. I didn't laugh back. 'Here, I'll get you up the stairs.'

She gripped the back of the wheelchair and looked around. 'Who are you with?'

That was the last straw. I yelled at her, 'I've been let out on my own for the day! And don't you touch this chair. You're too old to pull it up those stairs. I don't want to be responsible for your heart attack '

She snapped her hands away from the chair as if she'd had an electric shock. 'Oh,' she said, weakly.

And suddenly, embarrassment upon embarrassment, my mother was there. Apologising for me once again.

'Where did you come from? Were you following me?'

She was blushing. Stammering out apologies and explanations. 'I was worried, James. I wouldn't have let you know, I just wanted to make sure you were all right.' She tried for a smile. 'Lucky I was here though, eh? Now I'll get you up these stairs and then I'll leave you. I promise.'

The librarian's voice was all concern once again. 'Is this his first time out on his own?'

If I could have run that old librarian over in my wheelchair then, I would have. I wanted to scream at her, 'I'm here! You can ask me!'

But what would be the use? They wouldn't listen. No one ever listened.

So in the end I had no choice. I allowed me and my chair to be hauled up the stairs to the library. I even managed a wry smile when I saw the notice above the front door. 'This entrance is not suitable for wheelchair access.'

I like it when they tell you, I thought.

My mother fussed around me, but finally left with a promise to come back in an hour to collect me. As if I was a parcel. What was the point of arguing? She'd only wait for me and follow me again if I said no.

'Now, can I get you a book, dear?' The librarian was still smiling, even after my mother had gone. But it was an effort for her. From being the poor little soul in the wheelchair, I had now become a bad-tempered boy who didn't appreciate his mother.

Good – I preferred to be treated that way. I answered in exactly her condescending tone. 'No, dear. I want to see all the newspapers from the first of June onwards.'

Her face pinched in annoyance. 'Wouldn't it be easier for you to go through them on the computer?'

Her voice was so patronising I could have screamed. 'No. I'm afraid I want the papers. In my hand. Here!' I slapped my hand on the table in front of me.

She waddled off, not a happy bunny, but I didn't care. It was always the same. Stick the boy in the wheelchair in front of the computer. He'll not get into any trouble there. Well, stuff that!

Her face was still screwed up when she brought the papers into the musty-smelling reading room and slammed them down on the table in front of me. I tutted at her, put my fingers to my lips then pointed to the sign on the wall. SILENCE.

Her eyes flashed. I half expected to see steam whooshing out of her ears at any minute. But she said nothing. Well, she wouldn't. Not to a poor boy in a wheelchair. It was amazing what I could get away with. She only turned with a sniff and padded softly back to her desk.

I hadn't realised how painful it would be reading about the accident for the first time.

TWO MEN DIE IN HEAD-ON COLLISION. BOY SERIOUSLY INJURED

One of those men had been my dad.

DRUNK DRIVER CAUSES DEATH ON MOTORWAY

So, he'd been drunk. And my mother thought I should feel sorry for him? I read on:

Sam Shearer (19) died when the van he was driving skidded out of control, veered on to the wrong side of the motorway and crashed into the Peugeot of the Gordon family, who were returning from holiday. The father, Donald Gordon, died instantly. His son, James, was seriously injured. The distraught mother, who walked away from the crash, sustaining only minor injuries, is being comforted by relatives.

Yes. She walked away. I'd never walk again. I'd never see my dad again.

All because of drunken Sam Shearer. I hated him. He hadn't lived so far away from us either, on one of the estates on the edge of town. I had probably passed him on the street at one time. Never knowing that one day he would change my whole life.

I turned to another paper. Another story.

But it never changed. Always the same ending.

My dad always died.

I couldn't walk.

This hadn't been a good idea, coming here. Reading all of this. My mother had been right to keep it all from me.

I turned yet another page. And there, right in front of me, was a photo of my dad.

DONALD GORDON: KILLED IN YESTERDAY'S CRASH

My dad, smiling, happy. One of our holiday snaps. I had taken that photograph. I could remember everything about that day. The sun, the fun, the laughter.

I couldn't take any more of this. I almost slammed the folder closed. Almost – but my eye was caught by another photograph.

And this photograph made my blood run cold, my hands shake. Took the breath from me.

It was a photograph of Sam Shearer. Young, fair, good-looking.

But definitely not the same man I had seen at the wheel of the van as it hurtled towards us that night.

Chapter 6

When my mother came for me, I was still shaking with shock.

'James, you look awful. I knew this would be too much for you.' She began to fuss around me. 'Did you choose a book?'

It was the librarian who answered for me, her face still pinched in disapproval. 'He was reading the old newspapers. Something in them upset him.'

My mother realised at once exactly what I'd been reading about.

'Oh, James, I wish you hadn't done that.' She squeezed my shoulder. She didn't understand, only thought she did.

I wanted to *make* her understand. 'Mum,' I said at last, 'the man in the paper. Sam Shearer . . . that's not the man who was driving.'

I saw her stiffen, as if she suddenly had a steel ruler instead of a spine. I watched as the 'not that again' look clouded her face.

I hurried on. 'It was a different man I saw. The man I saw in the hospital that day – that was the driver. Not that Sam Shearer. Honest.'

She glanced around to make sure no one was listening to us. By this time the librarian had moved back to the counter. 'James, you're mistaken. It was raining. It was dark. You couldn't possibly have seen the other driver. Do you know what you went through that night? Hell. That's what you went through. You can't possibly be sure. Sam Shearer *was* the other driver. And he's dead. Whatever else you think you saw was only in your imagination.'

She wouldn't listen any more. There was no point in arguing.

Yet, as we made our way home, it was all I could think about. I couldn't be wrong. I knew what I had seen.

I had wanted her to go to the police, tell them about it. But I saw almost at once it would be useless. She didn't believe me. Neither would they. No one would listen to me. Everything was against me.

They wouldn't listen because my memory was unreliable after all I'd been through.

They wouldn't listen because I was just a boy.

And, most importantly, they wouldn't listen to me because I was in a wheelchair.

I spent the next few days feeling more miserable than ever. It hadn't been Sam Shearer I had seen. I knew that. And nothing was going to convince me otherwise.

But how was I ever going to prove it?

And then it came to me. Surely his family would help? They wouldn't want their son to go on being thought of as a murderer? Surely, if anyone was going to listen to me, to believe me, it would be Sam Shearer's family?

He had lived on the estate on the edge of the town. Although I didn't know the exact address, I looked up the name in the phone book. Shearer. There were only five in the whole area.

However, it took me another two days to pluck up the courage to actually call.

What would I say?

What *could* I say?

The first Shearer I phoned turned out to be an old woman who mistook me for the plumber. I had to promise to come and unblock her drain before she would let me go.

The second was a morose man who slammed down the phone because I had woken him out of a nightshift sleep.

It was third time lucky.

A man's voice answered after the fourth ring. 'Aye?'

I couldn't stop my voice from shaking as I asked, 'Is that Sam Shearer's house?'

There was a hesitation. 'Who's this?'

The man could tell that mine was only a boy's voice. I tried to sound more mature, more sure of myself. 'Sam Shearer was your son?'

There was a pause and when he answered this time, he sounded apprehensive. 'So? What do you want?'

I was sure he was going to hang up on me and I didn't want that. The words began tumbling out of me. 'Mr Shearer, don't hang up. This is James Gordon. The boy who was in the crash that your son –'

The phone was slammed down before I could say anything else. I waited, praying that he'd dial 1471 and call back. Angry at myself. I should have thought it out more carefully. But I knew Sam Shearer's family was the only link I had to the truth, and I wasn't going to let it go. I decided I would give it five minutes and try again.

It was only three minutes later when the phone rang shrilly. I snatched it up eagerly. Hoping it was Sam Shearer's dad phoning back.

It wasn't.

'Just what's your game?' The girl's voice was harsh and angry. 'My dad's really upset because of you. What do you mean, phoning here?'

'Look, my name's James Gordon –'

She didn't let me get anything else out. 'So? What right do you have to phone my dad? It wasn't his fault what happened.' I tried to get a word in. This girl wouldn't let me. 'My big brother died as well, you know. I don't expect you to have any sympathy about that. Because he killed your dad and you're in a wheelchair – and it's all his fault and my dad's got to live with that. So we don't need you calling up and harassing us. And if you call here again, I'll come round to your house and thump you!'

I was growing more angry with every word. How dare she talk to me like this? I hadn't done anything wrong.

'Do you hear me, moron?'

'You're the moron,' I snapped back at her. 'And, actually, I was phoning to say it wasn't your brother's fault. He wasn't driving that night.'

Then *I* slammed the phone down. My heart was beating so fast. No one had spoken to me like that in ages. Everyone pussyfooted around me these days. And this . . . moron . . . had the cheek to bawl me out. After all, I was the one in the wheelchair. I was the victim here. The more I thought about it, the angrier I became. The phone rang again, ten minutes later. But I didn't answer it. I'd had enough for one day.

Kirsty put the phone down. The moron was probably too scared to pick up. Had she heard him right? 'Your brother wasn't driving that night.'

She stood up and walked into the kitchen. Her dad was in there, pretending to stare out of the window. He turned as he heard her come in.

'Dad, that boy said –'

He brushed her words away. He didn't want to listen. Didn't ever want to talk about it. They'd had lots of horrible calls after the accident. People screaming down the line about the terrible thing Sam had done. Making their awful situation almost unbearable. Finally, they had stopped and Kirsty had hoped it was all over. This had been the first in such a long time.

'Listen, sweetheart. Your old dad's just going out for a breath of fresh air, OK?' He smiled at her. Ruffled her hair as he went past.

'Will you back for your tea, Dad?'

He assured her he would. But he wouldn't. And the only fresh air he would be enjoying would be on the way to the nearest pub.

'Your brother wasn't driving that night.'

The words echoed over and over again in her mind. And she knew she just couldn't let them go. She was going to have to find out more.

The next day was Saturday. Not that it made much difference to me. One day was pretty much like another. I lay along the sofa watching some grotty old film. Football on the other side, but I never watched it now. My mother was in the kitchen, scrubbing out her oven. It was amazing the boring things she could find to do in that kitchen. I heard the doorbell. Listened to my mother's footsteps as she padded down the hall. I wasn't much interested. It wouldn't be for me. It never was these days.

This time I was wrong.

My mother popped her head round the door. She looked puzzled, but pleased.

'James, you've got a visitor.'

A girl stepped in behind her. Skinny, with a toothy grin and sandy-coloured hair that looked as if she'd been caught in a high wind.

'This is Kirsty . . .' My mum looked at the girl, waiting for a surname.

Kirsty obliged with a smile. 'Kirsty Lewis.'

'Kirsty Lewis,' my mother repeated to me as if I hadn't heard her. 'Kirsty's come along from her church group. They have a youth centre and they're looking for new members. Isn't that nice, James?'

Kirsty stepped forward boldly. 'I hope you don't mind me coming, James.' She had a sickly-sweet little voice that matched her smile.

I watched her warily. I didn't need anyone to play games with. Least of all a girl. And I certainly didn't need to be entertained. I didn't say that, but it all showed plainly on my face.

Mum looked wary too for a second. 'Mind you, I hope you're not visiting strange houses on your own.'

'Of course not, Mrs Gordon. We've always got a responsible adult with us.' She waved a hand to some invisible person out in the street. 'They know exactly where I am.'

Responsible adult! She talked as if she was an old granny.

'I tell you what,' Mum turned to Kirsty, 'why don't I get you both some juice and crisps?'

Kirsty Lewis beamed an enthusiastic smile. 'That would be lovely, Mrs Gordon.'

'You two get to know each other. I won't be a minute.' My mother left the room, closing the door gently behind her.

Kirsty Lewis turned to me and her smile disappeared. So did her syrupy-sweet voice. 'Right, moron. What did you mean, my brother wasn't driving that night?'

Chapter 7

My hair practically stood on end in surprise. 'It's you!' I said. The moron I'd spoken to on the phone. Sam Shearer's sister. I could hardly believe that she'd had the nerve to come here to my house, to lie to my mother. To pretend to be some kind of good Samaritan. This girl was scary.

'Yes, it's me.' She threw herself down on the sofa beside me. 'Had to come, didn't I? You wouldn't answer the phone.'

'You lied to my mum.' I still couldn't take in her cheek.

She just shrugged her shoulders. 'Not really. I am in a church youth club. And Lewis is my middle name. So, right,' she said, getting straight to the point. 'What was the idea, phoning my house?' She certainly wasn't wasting any time.

I just stared at her, couldn't say a word.

That annoyed her. 'Suddenly, you've lost your voice. It was working OK when you phoned my dad.' She moved her face so close to mine I thought she was going to eat me. 'Right then, what did you mean – it wasn't my brother's fault?'

I was saved by my mother, skipping in, carrying a tray with Coke and crisps and biscuits. She hesitated after putting the tray down on the coffee table, dying to stay and find out all about this stranger. 'You two getting to know each other?'

Kirsty smiled sweetly. She answered in her matching voice. 'We're getting on dead good, Mrs Gordon.' She fluttered her eyelashes at me. I thought I was going to be sick. 'Aren't we, James?'

I still couldn't say a word. I had never come across anyone before who could lie like this Kirsty.

My mother gave in, and moved reluctantly to the door. 'And exactly what church do you belong to, Kirsty?'

'St Bride's,' Kirsty said at once. Surely not a lie this time.

I saw my mother's face fall. 'St Bride's. Isn't that over near the big estate?' Bad area, notorious for gangs and trouble. Always made the headlines in the local paper.

Kirsty nodded. Then added reassuringly, 'But we've got a great minister. And the youth centre is brilliant. There's a disco and games and we have outings. I thought James could come along.'

Already my mother was shaking her head. 'Oh, I don't know. It's away on the other side of town. I don't think I could allow that.'

That discussion alone decided me. I wasn't having my fate decided by two females. 'I'd like to go,' I said, though I already hated the thought of going anywhere with Kirsty.

Kirsty added enthusiastically, 'We've got special transport for wheelchairs, Mrs Gordon. We could pick him up and drop him back home. I could arrange it.'

I was beginning to get angry now. 'You make me sound like litter,' I snapped.

Kirsty turned to me and giggled. 'That's a good one. Are you always this funny?'

Even my mother smiled. She had warmed to Kirsty. 'Well, I suppose if I checked it all out first, it would be all right, eh, James?'

I flicked up the volume on the remote control. 'Depends. I'll see what they've got to offer first. Don't want to waste my time with a bunch of religious morons.'

My mother gasped. 'James!' She was all apologies to Kirsty. 'I'm so sorry, Kirsty.'

Kirsty didn't stop smiling. She looked like a saint. All she needed was a halo to materialise above her head. 'Oh, I understand, Mrs Gordon. It doesn't sound like fun, but I'm sure James would enjoy it when he meets all my friends.'

Even I would have believed her, if I hadn't known any better. She sounded so plausible and genuine.

Kirsty changed from Dr Jekyll back to Mr Hyde as soon as the door closed behind my mother. 'Are you always this nasty?' she said.

'Always.'

She just shrugged. ''S OK. So am I.'

She began to unwrap a chocolate biscuit.

'OK, tell me what you meant about our Sam.'

She hadn't been the one I wanted to tell. She couldn't help me. She was as young as I was, and a girl. What could she possibly do to help me find the truth? Yet perhaps she could convince her father, and he would do something about it.

So I began to tell her the whole story, about seeing the man in the hospital, about the dream, my visit to the library and the photograph that had shocked me. The photograph of her brother.

'But that wasn't who I saw driving that night. Not your brother. The guy who was driving was the one I saw at the hospital, and don't you try to say I'm mistaken. Everybody else has.'

She licked the chocolate from her third biscuit off her fingers. 'I'm not going to say that. I want you to be right. My brother was great, used to come to the youth centre, never got into any trouble   till he got in with some bad people. One in particular.'

'The one I saw at the hospital?' I asked hopefully. Because if it was, maybe we could speak to the police. Surely they couldn't ignore both of us.

'Describe him again.'

I tried, but description isn't my strong point. 'Kind of fair hair. Floppy. Wild eyes.'

She curled up her lip in disgust. 'It could be anybody. Could be you, especially the wild eyes.'

I shrugged. 'I'll know him when I see him.'

She seemed to be thinking over something while she got stuck into yet another biscuit. 'It could be Eric Bethel,' she said at last.

'Eric Bethel? Who's he?'

'Bad trouble, that's what he is. He's the one who got Sam into all sorts of nasty stuff. He used to go to the youth centre as well, until they realised he was only using the centre to sell things he shouldn't have been selling. Then Donny barred him.' She nodded. 'Bet it's him. I know he saw Sam that night. But the police questioned him and he said he left Sam earlier. Didn't see him again. But then, he wouldn't tell the truth, would he?'

I was getting excited. Could this Eric Bethel be the one I had seen? It seemed more than likely to me.

'Don't you see? If he's as bad as you say, he could have been driving, he could have caused the accident. Then just left your Sam to take the blame.'

Kirsty looked at me as if I was an idiot. 'And walked away from a crash like that without a scratch?'

I stared right back at her. 'My mother did,' I said.

She didn't flinch. 'Does that bother you?' she asked.

This time I couldn't hold her gaze. 'No,' I lied. 'I'm, just saying it's possible.' I was grateful she didn't follow that up.

'The last person who's supposed to have seen Sam that night is his girlfriend, Lynn. She said he was pretty drunk and she couldn't stop him from driving.'

'Is there any way you can talk to this Lynn?'

'I'll see Lynn at the youth centre. She's thick as a brick, but she might be able to tell me something.'

I didn't like the way this was going. 'No way, pal. She might be able to tell *us* something. *We'll* go and talk to her at this youth centre. You're not taking this over by yourself.'

Kirsty stared at me open-mouthed. 'And how am I supposed to get you to the youth centre?'

I mimicked her sickly, syrupy-sweet voice. 'We've got special transport. We could pick him up and drop him back home . . .' I let that sink in. 'So do it.'

Kirsty sneered right back at me. 'I don't think I like you very much.'

Chapter 8

My mother couldn't have been more excited, or anxious or worried or happy, if it had been my wedding day.

For half an hour before it was due to arrive, she stood at the window watching for the centre's van.

'And Kirsty said it will bring you home too, didn't she?'

I didn't bother to answer. My mother had double-checked and treble-checked all the details herself. She had phoned the centre to speak to the caretaker, a Mr Blackett. The minister was off at some kind of conference, but Mr Blackett had filled her in with all the details about the centre itself, assured her the van was fitted for a wheelchair. I had been angry about that. 'And I suppose you told everybody who I was and what happened to me? Poor James Gordon. So now they'll feel sorry for me.'

I had warned her over and over not to say who I was. Not just because I didn't want any pity. But also because there would be a lot of questions asked if anyone found out that James Gordon and Sam Shearer's sister had got together.

'Oh no, dear. I had to tell them your name, but I didn't tell them how exactly you got your injuries. But you have to understand how I feel, James. I can't just let you go off anywhere, with anyone. And that youth centre is right on the edge of a horrible estate. Anybody could go there.'

And anyone did, if the reputation of Eric Bethel was to be believed.

'You don't have to worry. I'm only going there once. To see what it's like.'

And I'd seen the dismay cloud her face. I knew she was torn between wanting me to go places with people my own age, and being afraid of letting me out of her sight.

I should understand, sympathise. But it only made me angry and resentful.

'I do like that Kirsty. I think she's a trustworthy girl.'

Oh yeah, Mum. I wished I could tell her exactly how trustworthy Kirsty really was. She hadn't even given her real name.

'Are you looking forward to going?' Mum asked.

I just grimaced and didn't answer. I didn't trust myself to say anything because, in fact, I *was* looking forward to it. Even if I had to go with the awful Kirsty. I was excited and apprehensive and frightened.

I never used to feel frightened. I had always been the one who stepped into trouble first. Hadn't Ash's dad once given me a terrible row for egging Ash on to join me too near a bonfire one Guy Fawkes night? We'd both ended up in hospital after a firework had exploded right by us. But I had always been the one to do what no one else dared. I did stuff first and thought later.

Now, I was scared.

'Here it comes.' My mother turned to me excitedly. 'And Kirsty's here too.' She added that as if I'd be delighted. I wasn't. I still wasn't sure what I thought of her. But circumstances had thrown us together and for the moment it seemed we were stuck with each other.

Mr Blackett was driving and he came in first, introducing himself to my mother. Assuring her that I would be well looked after. He turned to me and smiled. 'So this is James,' he said. And he held out his hand for me to shake. 'You'll enjoy yourself, son.'

Behind him, Kirsty bounced in, all smiles. Sweetness itself. Why couldn't my mother see through her? And she wasn't alone. She had brought two of her friends with her. I cringed with embarrassment. It was bad enough to be going somewhere with one girl in tow, but three?

'Hello, Mrs Gordon. This is Gemma.' Gemma's teeth were too big and she smiled too much. She grinned now at my mum.

'Pleased to meet you, Mrs Gordon.'

Kirsty pulled her other friend into view. She seemed to be more interested in her reflection in the mirror. She had two ponytails bobbing about on either side of her head. She looked stupid. 'This is Leanne.'

If Gemma smiled too much, Leanne was a giggler. 'Hi.' She waved a greeting at my mother. 'Oh, this is a lovely house, Mrs Gordon. I've always wanted to live in a bungalow.' Then she went into a fit of the giggles. To my surprise, my mother seemed to be delighted by the giggles, and all the girls.

'Aren't these three lovely girls, James?' she asked.

Wrong question.

'I thought there were only two ugly sisters.' And that was definitely the wrong answer.

Kirsty put on her vomiting sweet voice and clucked with adult disapproval. 'What are we going to do with him, Mrs Gordon?'

I felt like ramming my wheelchair into her, but for now I had to keep my mouth shut. Pretend at least I could stand her. 'Come on, Kirsty.' I said it as if she was my best friend. 'I want to get going.'

Mr Blackett was already outside, lowering the ramp which lifted my wheelchair into the van. My mother went over, again, exactly when I would be home, and what to do in case of an emergency.

'Are you sure you don't want to come?' Mr Blackett asked her.

She would have loved to have come. She glanced at me, but she could see by my thunderous look that was the last thing I wanted.

'Oh no, James has got his mobile with him if he needs me.'

She stood waving till the van turned the corner. Kirsty kept her smile in place for the same time. As soon as it was safe, her sickly smile became a sneer. 'You're really horrible to your mother. I don't know how she puts up with you.'

'I think it's called guilt,' I answered in a surly voice.

Kirsty thought about that for a moment. 'What's she got to feel guilty about?' she asked.

I said nothing. If she needed an answer to that one, she was even stupider than she looked.

Instead I snapped, 'What did you bring them along for?'

Leanne and Gemma gasped in unison. 'Them, indeed! There are boys who would just love to be in our company.'

'I know, the daftest ones in your school, probably,' I snapped back.

Leanne opened her mouth so wide I thought she might swallow herself. I wished. She shook her head and her ponytails wiggled with a life of their own. 'See, you, James Gordon, you are really nasty.'

'You're too nice, Kirsty,' Gemma told her. 'I don't know how you can be bothered with him.'

'I'm just trying to get another badge for the Guides. My "Be Nice to Someone Horrible for a Week" badge.'

Kirsty was a Guide as well? Now she really *was* scary.

Suddenly they were all giggling as if I wasn't there.

Mr Blackett glanced at me in his mirror. 'You're outnumbered, son.' He grinned. And the girls suddenly remembered he was there and jumped at him to change his Classic fm to Radio One.

'I thought they would be good cover,' Kirsty explained when she knew Gemma and Leanne couldn't hear.

'You're talking like a secret agent.' She really was annoying me now.

'Well, we are kinda undercover. Be honest. You can't let anybody know who you are, and I can't let your mother know who I am. And we're going to dig out a secret. I think it's quite exciting.'

'They don't know who I am, do they?' I nodded in the direction of her two friends.

'Of course they don't. They just think I'm doing a good deed. I'm such a good person, you see.'

She said it as if she actually believed it was true.

Her voice became a whisper. 'I've been thinking – what does it matter to you whether our Sam was innocent or not?'

I looked at her as if she was daft. 'I don't care about your brother. But he wasn't the one driving the van that night, and I'm not going to let the guy who *was* driving get away with killing my dad. I want revenge, right?'

I said it with such bitterness that even Kirsty didn't answer for a while. It was only as the van was drawing to a halt at the centre that she said with just as much bitterness, 'And I'm not going to let him get away with blaming our Sam for it. He's ruined our lives as well.'

I looked at her then, as if for the first time. Not as the mouthy moron, Kirsty, who had lied to my mother, but as an ally. The only one I had. We were partners now – and we were going to find out the truth together.

Chapter 9

I hadn't imagined that people went to youth clubs any more, but this place – the youth centre – was buzzing. Boys and girls played on the pool tables, or at the pinball machines. There were others playing table tennis, and in a separate room I could see the flashing lights of a disco, could feel the beat of the music throbbing through my chair.

A fresh-faced young man bounded towards us as soon as we came in. He was wearing a long cardigan and a grin. 'So this is James?' he said enthusiastically. 'Our Kirsty here has told us all about you. You're cousins, I believe.'

I flushed and was sure, no matter how stupid this Cardigan looked, he had to see that I was embarrassed because it was all such a lie! Kirsty just smiled.

'I'm Pat,' the young man beamed. 'Standing in for Donny while he's at the conference.'

I remembered Kirsty talking about Donny who was, I presumed, the minister.

'Welcome to our youth centre,' he went on brightly. 'I do hope you come again. Now . . .' he looked around. Spotted another boy the same age as me. He was fat and spotty and looked sulky. He was in a wheelchair too. 'Come and meet Peter,' he said.

It was Kirsty who spoke up. 'Why would he want to meet that drip? He's the most boring person I've ever come across.'

I could answer that. 'Because he's in a wheelchair too. So we're bound to have something in common, that right?'

Pat the Cardigan looked flustered. 'No, of course I didn't mean that . . .' He tried to think of what he did mean. Couldn't come up with anything. 'Trust you, Kirsty.'

Kirsty was obviously well known as 'the mouth'.

'Come on, Jamesie. We'll go into the disco.'

She swaggered past and beckoned to me to follow.

'Jamesie!' I yelled after her. 'Who do you think you're calling Jamesie?'

But I was glad she had said what she did to the Cardigan. Glad that at least somebody understood. Everybody always tried to put me with someone else who was disabled. It was the thing that annoyed me more than anything else.

The disco was too loud, too noisy and too crowded. As the music hit her, Kirsty began to sway and strut to the rhythm. 'Lynn Mitchell might be in here,' she mouthed to me, then turned her head back to the crowd.

'I can't see a thing!' I yelled. But it was impossible to make myself heard. Impossible for me to see anyone above the crowd. I began to grow frustrated. As Kirsty moved forward, hypnotised by the beat, I stayed at the back. If only I could follow her. People kept stepping against me, looking down apologetically, then ignoring me. I was afraid. No. Not quite afraid. But I felt vulnerable.

Kirsty, caught up totally in the music by this time, was moving away from me, feet tapping, hips swaying. I wanted to call after her, but I knew she'd never hear.

Suddenly, a jacket landed on my lap. A moment later a coat joined it. I looked up. A boy and girl just coming into the disco had mistaken me for an empty chair. 'Do you mind?' I shouted at them, but they didn't hear. They were already nuzzling each other and dancing to the music. And, besides, nobody could hear anything above that grinding, throbbing music. 'If anybody throws another coat on me, I'll run them over!' I challenged those in the vicinity. They ignored me. I realised I could say anything. Insult anyone. I yelled across to a particularly hard-looking boy leaning against the wall. 'Hey you, ugly mug. Yeah, you! Try that again, pal, and I'll roast you over a slow fire. OK, who wants a fight?' I raised my fists like a boxer, pretending I was chewing gum, looking tough. But the anger was leaving me. Even now, the idea was making me giggle. 'I should charge. I could make a fortune as a mobile cloakroom.'

It was just then I noticed that Kirsty was watching me as if I'd gone bonkers. 'Are you talking to yourself?' she bent right down to me and asked.

'It's the only way I can get a sensible conversation.'

She leaned close to my ear and bellowed so loudly it sent a tickle down my spine. 'I've just seen Lynn Mitchell. C'mon. Jamesie.'

There she went with the Jamesie again. But before I could answer her she was off, pushing her way through the crowd, expecting me to do the same.

Chapter 10

I don't know how I had thought Lynn Mitchell might look, but she was nothing like I expected. Thick as a brick, Kirsty had called her. I suppose I had expected her to look stupid too.

She was leaning across a table and from the back she had a slim, shapely figure tightly encased in her jeans. Kirsty called out to her, and when she turned round her long blonde hair moved with her and her green eyes smiled. She was gorgeous.

'Hi, Kirsty, how are you?'

Kirsty got straight to the point. 'Me and Jamesie have got to talk to you, Lynn.'

Lynn shook her head and covered her ears. 'Can't hear you,' she mouthed. She pointed out of the disco. 'Come on.' As she wiggled her way out, I noticed the eyes of every boy at the table followed her. I didn't blame them.

'You comin' back, Lynn?' one of them shouted. But she didn't hear, or perhaps she ignored them.

I followed on after her. I could not take my eyes off her bottom.

Kirsty, walking beside me, noticed and gave me a push that almost sent me flying out of my chair. 'What do you think you're lookin' at?' she bellowed in my ear.

'I can't help it. It's at eye level with me. I've got to look at it.'

'You don't have to enjoy it so much,' she said, sticking her tongue out at me.

Outside, in the relative quiet of the games room, Lynn turned back to us and seemed surprised to find me still there. She went down a little in my estimation then.

Wiggling bottom or not. Like everyone else, she hadn't noticed me. I was in a wheelchair. I was invisible.

'This is Jamesie,' Kirsty told her. 'He's with me.'

She placed a hand on my shoulder as if I was her best pal . . . or maybe just her pet monkey.

Lynn smiled down at me, then her eyes immediately moved back to Kirsty. 'So, what do you want to talk to me about?'

Just as I was beginning to think that they were going to talk over my head, Kirsty crouched down beside me so that her face was level with mine. Suddenly it was Lynn who was at the disadvantage. 'Me and Jamesie don't think our Sam was driving the van that night. We think he met up with somebody else and that's who was driving.'

So much for being subtle.

Lynn's face grew pale. 'What makes you think that?'

'Could somebody else have been driving, Lynn? You were the last to see him.'

Lynn didn't quite answer that. 'I wish you wouldn't torture yourself, Kirsty. This has been so hard for your dad.'

'Surely it would help if he knew his son hadn't been driving that night?' I said. Lynn looked at me, as if for the first time.

'But he was. I hate to say it. Wish it wasn't true, but I saw him go off in the van. He was driving. And he was drunk. I couldn't stop him.' Her green eyes were filling up. I was suddenly afraid she might be about to cry.

'He might have met somebody else after he left you,' Kirsty said.

'Like who?' It seemed to me then that Lynn was nervous. She kept swallowing and licking her lips. 'Who else do you mean?'

Kirsty shrugged. 'He met Eric Bethel as well that night, before he met you. Do you think Eric Bethel might have seen him afterwards?'

This time, I thought that Lynn Mitchell looked frightened. 'You keep back from Eric Bethel. That's what Sam should have done.'

'Wouldn't do any harm to talk to him.'

Now Lynn looked even more alarmed. 'Don't you go near him, Kirsty.'

Why, I wondered, was everyone so scared of this Eric Bethel?

'We're not blaming him for anything,' Kirsty said.

Not yet, I thought.

'We'll be really subtle,' she went on.

I almost laughed. Kirsty, subtle?

'Leave it be, Kirsty.' Lynn looked down at me. 'And you too. Sad as it is, Sam *was* driving that night. You'll just have to accept that. I was the last one to see him and he was driving. Right!' Lynn snapped the words out as if she was really annoyed. Then, with a flick of her blonde mane, she wiggled off, back to the boys who were awaiting her with their tongues hanging out. I could understand that feeling. My tongue was hanging out too.

'Well,' Kirsty said, 'what rattled her cage?'

'Maybe she's just scared of this Eric Bethel,' I said. 'Everybody else seems to be.'

'She's scared – that's for sure. She knows something, Jamesie. Something she isn't telling us,' Kirsty said, mysteriously. She was beginning to sound like a TV detective. At that moment, she noticed I still hadn't taken my eyes off Lynn Mitchell, and she gave me a punch. 'Typical!' she fumed. 'You can't see beyond a bottom and blonde hair.'

I laughed. 'So? What's wrong with that?'

Kirsty tried to flick her hair just like Lynn had. With the fright-night hairdo she had, it just didn't work. 'I expect to be appreciated for more than that,' she said.

This time I guffawed with laughter. 'You've not even got that to begin with.'

Kirsty gave me an even harder push. 'I will,' she said with confidence, 'but I want to be appreciated for my good nature.'

She was getting better by the minute, I thought. 'Try again, Kirsty. You're bound to come up with something you could be appreciated for.'

'Very funny.' And she was off again, leaving me with no option but to follow her. She really was annoying. She seemed to forget I was in a wheelchair and it wasn't as easy for me to wind my way through a crowd.

And, suddenly, it struck me. Wasn't that exactly what I wanted? For people to forget I was in a wheelchair?

'So, what's our next move?' I asked her. 'I'd like to see this Eric Bethel.'

She nodded. 'Exactly what I was thinking. You'll have to see him and then you'll know he's the one you're looking for. I'll find out where he hangs out, OK?' She stopped and lifted one of the table-tennis bats. 'Fancy a game?'

'Me and you?' I was surprised.

She looked around her dramatically. 'And who else would I be talking to, lame brain?' She shoved the bat at me. 'Come on,' she said.

I had enjoyed playing table tennis once. Used to be quite good at it. But I'd never played since the accident. And I'd certainly never played in a wheelchair. Perhaps I would embarrass myself in front of all these people. But when I looked around, it seemed no one was particularly interested. As for Kirsty, it didn't seem to occur to her. Probably thought she'd win anyway.

She didn't. I thrashed her in all three games we played. I did tribal yells of triumph after every win while Kirsty just got madder and madder.

'Stupid game!' she said, throwing her bat on the table with such force it actually bounced. Then she lifted her nose in the air. 'I let you win, you know.'

I whizzed my chair in front of her. 'You wouldn't spit on me if I was on fire. You're hardly likely to let me win at table tennis.'

I had to put up with the company of the grinning Gemma and the wobbly Leanne on the ride home. I was never so glad I wasn't a girl. It must be awful to be that stupid.

I was home before I had a chance to go over the events of the evening. My mother was waiting impatiently by the front door when I arrived, and asked so many questions and fussed over me so much that my good mood almost evaporated.

Good mood? It had been such a long time since I'd been in a good mood I'd almost forgotten what it was like.

I'd enjoyed the evening. I'd forgotten, just for a little while, that I was in a wheelchair. I'd played table tennis, argued with Kirsty and played detective too. I'd also met the beautiful Lynn. Wow!

And Kirsty was coming in the morning to discuss our next move. We were going to see this Eric Bethel and, according to Kirsty, he had to be the one who had been driving that night. And if he was, and he was as bad as everyone said, how on earth was I going to prove it?

As I went to sleep that night I realised that for the first time since the accident, I was actually looking forward to tomorrow.

The first thing Kirsty did when she got home was check if her dad had taken the meal she had left in the microwave. He hadn't. So he hadn't been in all day. She flopped on to the sofa. James had been really nasty to his mum when they had arrived back at his place, and it was clear she had been dying for him to come home. Desperate to know how he had got on. And James had snapped at her, and hardly answered.

If only he knew how lucky he was. Nowadays, she never had anyone waiting at home for her. Dad was never there.

There was no point going to bed. She knew she wouldn't sleep. So she lay on the sofa, pulled the duvet over her and waited for her dad.

Chapter 11

'Hello, Kirsty!' Mum greeted her so warmly Kirsty must have felt the heat. She liked Kirsty. Liked the fact she was coming to see her son. Her poor son in a wheelchair. She wouldn't have cared if she'd come from another planet and had two heads. She would still have welcomed her in. 'Would you like some Coke, some crisps?'

Kirsty, the walking waste-disposal unit, didn't have to be asked twice. In fact, when they came, she munched into my crisps as well.

'Do you think your mother would let you go to the shopping precinct with me?' she asked me as soon as we were alone.

'Today? To the precinct? With you?' I thought about that for a minute. 'On the one hand she'd be delighted I'm actually going anywhere. On the other, she'd probably follow us in the car.' I began to feel that frustrated annoyance grow in me again. Why should I not go to the precinct, with or without Kirsty? I used to. Before. 'Anyway, why do you want to go there?'

'Eric Bethel,' Kirsty said at once. 'That's where he hangs out. You have to see him. I want to talk to him. He's usually out of his face but we could interrogate him.'

'Interrogate him! You're talking as if we're the Secret Police.' She was unbelievable. 'You really think he's the one, don't you?'

I'd never seen her look so serious. 'He has to be. It couldn't be anybody else. It's all so clear to me. Sam met up with Eric after he left Lynn. Eric drove the van. He caused the crash. Eric Bethel's just the type who would let our Sam take the blame. And Lynn Mitchell knows it and she's too afraid to say anything.'

'You've tied up all the loose ends nicely, I see.'

She had made up her mind. I wasn't so sure. I had to see this Eric Bethel for myself. I so wanted to go to the precinct. But there was a part of me that didn't want to be seen in public. Not in a wheelchair. I still wasn't used to it. There would be people in the precinct. Especially on a Saturday. People my own age. People I knew. I wasn't sure if I could handle it.

Kirsty saw my hesitation and shrugged her shoulders. ''S all right. I'll just go myself. I don't really need you there. I'll bring you a photo of Eric Bethel.'

That was all I needed, and she knew it. 'No way. You're not going anywhere without me. This is my mystery, sister.'

It turned out to be a real struggle to convince my mother to let me go, however.

Kirsty did her best to assure her I would be safe with her. Safe with Kirsty? The mind boggled.

'We'll only be going to the record shop, Mrs Gordon. Maybe in for a hamburger. And Gemma and Leanne are meeting us there.'

I almost yelled. She hadn't told me I would have to suffer them too.

'I'll be with him all the time.'

I felt like kicking her. *I'll be with him all the time.* As if I was a baby who needed looking after. If only my mother knew. Kirsty would most probably walk five paces ahead and expect me to follow.

Mum finally gave in, but only if she could take us both there in the car and pick us up again. 'Call me on your mobile phone if you need me. You promise?'

My mum was pale with nerves as she left us at the entrance to the precinct. Kirsty smiled understandingly 'Honest, Mrs Gordon. I'll look after him.'

She was so sweet she could give you diabetes, I thought. Like one of those awful little girls in old-fashioned story books. Except for the hair. She still looked as if she had just woken up from a nightmare.

As soon as my mother had gone, I snapped back at her. 'I don't need anybody to look after me, right?'

Yet, I had to admit, I couldn't have done it without Kirsty beside me – or usually beside me.

One minute I was talking to her about Eric Bethel and the next she was off to look in a shop window.

'Look at that dress. It is absolutely beautiful.'

She was admiring a bit of cotton that definitely needed ironing.

I whizzed over beside her. 'Look at the price,' I said. 'There's hardly enough material there to blow your nose.'

'You have no taste, James Gordon,' she answered me, and then she was off to another window to gaze at something even more awful.

'Hey, you're supposed to be looking after me, remember?' I called, following behind her.

She put on one of her funny faces. 'You don't need anybody to look after you. You said so yourself.'

I ignored that. 'When are we going to see this Eric Bethel?' I asked.

She didn't get a chance to answer. Suddenly the giggling and screaming hyenas who were Leanne and Gemma rushed up and engulfed her in hugs and kisses as if they hadn't seen her for years.

'Know who we've just seen?' Leanne shrieked. 'That big, really good-looking guy who plays in the school football team. And he noticed me.' I wasn't surprised. Leanne now had three ponytails on top of her head and they had been sprayed with three different colours of glitter. He would have to have been blind not to notice her.

Then her ponytails started waving about all over the place as if they had come alive. Leanne was jumping about and screaming.

'He noticed me! And he is *gorgeous*!'

Both Gemma and Kirsty thought this was wonderful. They started screaming too. Then they squealed, 'Leanne's having a wobbly! Leanne's having a wobbly!'

I was mega embarrassed. I hoped that for once I *was* invisible.

Then they started admiring each other's clothes. It was just getting worse and worse.

'Do you like my new shoes?' Gemma held out her feet for their inspection. 'Just bought them.'

'They are brilliant, Gemma.'

The shoes were awful. They looked like something Frankenstein would wear.

'Do you like my hair? I've just had it done.' Leanne flicked her ponytails at me.

'You want to have your hairdresser arrested,' I told her.

Kirsty gave me a shove. 'Don't listen to him, Leanne. It's absolutely lovely.'

And they all giggled and laughed and screamed.

I realised then there are worse things than being in a wheelchair.

Leanne bent right down to me. 'No, be honest, Jamesie. From a boy's point of view, do you think my hair's gorgeous or what?'

Once again she flicked a ponytail right in my face. 'You'd be better-looking bald,' I told her. Well, she did ask me to be honest.

Suddenly, to my complete and utter embarrassment, I saw my two friends, Paul and Ash, coming towards us. I felt my face go red. They phoned me regularly. I never answered their calls. They were always asking me to go to the precinct with them. I always refused. Now here I was . . . and I was with a bunch of giggling girls.

They stopped right in front of us, and seemed astonished to find me there. 'Where's your mum?' Ash asked, looking around for her.

'I'm not with my mum.' And I knew I sounded annoyed. I didn't mean it to come out like that.

'You could have come here with us,' Paul said.

But I could never do that. Didn't they realise how painful that would be for me? They could walk. They could run. I couldn't.

So I retreated, as I always did, into a moody, unpleasant retort. 'Hate this place. It's a dump. It's got worse.'

At this insult to her favourite haunt, Kirsty turned right round. 'What do you mean, it's a dump? This is a brilliant precinct. Isn't it, girls?'

Leanne and Gemma readily agreed. They began to list its benefits, finger by finger. 'It's got dress shops and accessory shops and shoe shops.'

'And cake shops,' Kirsty added, always thinking of her stomach.

'It's got record shops,' Leanne said. 'And the Hamburger Palace.'

Gemma spoke to Paul. 'That's where we're going. Want to come?'

Paul looked at me in disbelief. 'Are you with them?'

More embarrassment when Kirsty answered, 'Actually, Jamesie's with me.'

I turned on her. 'I am not with you—'

Ash burst out laughing. 'Jamesie?'

This was getting worse by the minute. I didn't know where to look.

'If I come for a hamburger,' Paul said to Gemma, 'are you paying?'

'It's supposed to be boys that pay,' Kirsty said.

That made all the boys laugh. 'In your dreams,' Ash said. 'This is the twenty-first century.'

And before I knew what was happening, it seemed that Paul and Ash were going for a hamburger with us. Although it was more as if they were being kidnapped. I didn't know how I felt about that. Pleased, and yet a bit afraid.

With Kirsty, however, I didn't have time to think about anything. She suddenly yanked me by the elbow. 'C'mon, Jamesie.' She called after her friends, 'Me and Jamesie are just going to look at something, right?'

Ash, who was being hauled along by Leanne, called after us. 'Hope it's not an engagement ring, Jamesie!'

Kirsty giggled and called after them, 'Get us a good seat, right?'

Then she was off, chewing her gum and slouching ahead of me. She was making me really angry. 'You call me "Jamesie" one more time and I'll run you over with this thing.'

She turned to me and pouted. 'I wouldn't have come with you if I'd known you were going to complain this much.'

'I've got every right to complain. I have never met anybody like you in my life.'

She threw her hands up dramatically and fluttered her eyelashes. 'There you are then. I'm a life-changing experience.'

'You are a nut,' I said, going after her again.

We turned the corner and she stopped so suddenly I almost did run into her. 'There he is, Jamesie,' she said, and her voice had changed. It was soft, quiet and fearful. 'There's Eric Bethel.'

I couldn't move. I could hardly look. A sudden awful feeling hit me. Was this the end of the trail? Was Eric Bethel the man I'd seen driving the van that night?

Chapter 12

I hovered beside Kirsty. I couldn't move. She turned to look at me. 'What's the problem?' she asked.

I swallowed. 'I'm frightened to look. If it is him, how are we going to prove it?'

'If it is him, and it probably is, we're going to the police. I'll tell my dad. He'll kill him. He's always hated Eric Bethel. If it wasn't for him, our Sam would have kept on going to the youth centre, he would have kept his job . . . he'd still be alive. If he's let our Sam get the blame for this, I'll kill him as well. I will, Jamesie. I will.'

When she spoke like that, with such real feeling, her thin face went pale. I thought that maybe this was the real Kirsty at last.

'There's only one way to find out,' and I wheeled ahead of her.

There was a crowd of young men standing around the record store. They were wearing trackies and baseball caps and they looked shifty, as if they were up to no good. Shoppers passing them gave them a wide berth and two security men didn't take their eyes off them once. My eyes scoured around, looking for that one familiar face. The only face I was interested in.

'There he is,' Kirsty said, pointing to one youth with his back to us. He was the only one wearing a leather jacket and jeans and he was bent over a girl who was grinning up at him. Kirsty called out to him, 'Eric! Hi!' She sounded pleased to see him. All the bitterness of a moment ago had gone.

Eric Bethel stood straight and turned at the sound of his name. The floppy fair hair hung around his face, his eyes had a wild, scary look about them. His skin was white and spotty and his ears stuck out. They were the only part of him with any colour, going bright red as he recognised Kirsty.

This was Eric Bethel. I let out a sigh. Almost, but not quite, the guy from the hospital. Almost, but not quite, the guy behind the wheel.

Kirsty looked straight at me. ''S'at him?' Her lips were pursed. I knew what she wanted the answer to be.

I shook my head. 'There must have been somebody else. Kind of fair hair, pale face.' I sounded as if I *was* describing Eric Bethel. His cold eyes, his white face. I could picture the man so clearly in my mind, but I could never seem to tell anyone exactly what he looked like.

'OK,' she said at once, as if she didn't quite believe me, 'but we still want to talk to him, don't we?'

'Yeah, of course.'

Eric Bethel was grinning at Kirsty as she moved towards him. 'What are you doing here?' he asked.

He hadn't noticed me yet, but I was used to that.

Kirsty got straight to the point as usual. 'What happened that last night you saw our Sam?'

Suddenly Eric Bethel looked annoyed. 'What are you bringing all that up for? I've had to go through this a hundred times. Lynn Mitchell saw him after I did. Ask her.'

I was getting annoyed at being ignored. I wheeled myself so close to Eric I almost rammed his toes.

Eric noticed I was there for the first time.

'This is James, by the way,' Kirsty told him bluntly.

His face went even whiter. He jammed a finger against me. 'Are you trying to blame me for something? I had nothin' to do with that. Sam Shearer was supposed to come back and collect me, and he never did.'

'What was he coming back for?' Kirsty asked.

Eric Bethel looked nervous at that. As if he'd said something he hadn't meant to. 'Nothin'. We were going to the disco, that's it. What are you askin' all these questions for?' His wild eyes narrowed. 'James? Wait a minute.' His eyes took in the wheelchair. 'You're the boy that was in that accident, aren't you?' He shook his head, taking it all in. He looked at Kirsty again. 'What are you two doing together? This is sick.'

'I saw who was driving the van that night. And it wasn't Kirsty's brother.' I swallowed. His face was so close I could smell his breath and it wasn't pleasant. 'I'm just trying to find out who it was.'

Eric Bethel's wild eyes stared into mine. 'Are you tryin' to say it was me? You try to make out I was driving, and I'll make you really sorry.' He bared his teeth at me. 'I'll be after you. Know what I mean? I'm not taking the blame for anythin'. I hear about you saying it was me and I'll come and get you, right?' His voice was getting louder and louder.

'What's going on here?' One of the security men moved in between us, and I was never so glad to see anyone in my life. 'You OK, son?' he asked me.

Eric Bethel flicked his hand against my shoulder as if he was brushing dandruff from my jacket. 'Sure, no problem here. Eh, son?'

Kirsty pulled me back. 'Come on, Jamesie.'

We moved off, and we could hear the security man telling Eric and his cronies to get out of the precinct. We didn't stop until we had turned the corner and were out of sight.

'He means that, by the way. He does go after people. Usually with a baseball bat,' Kirsty said. 'Are you sure it wasn't him?'

'I wish it was,' I told her, 'but that's not who I saw at the hospital either.'

'It must have rattled him, seeing me and you together.'

'He's the only one who recognised me anyway. Lynn didn't.'

Kirsty shrugged. 'Thick as a brick. I told you.'

I caught up with her. 'He's hiding something as well. I wonder where he and your brother were supposed to be going. Not a disco, I'll bet. But how are we ever going to find out?'

Kirsty thought about that. 'They were probably up to no good. He was always getting Sam involved in something fishy. Maybe Lynn knows about it and Eric's threatened her as well, and that's why she's scared.'

'I think we should talk to her again.'

'You just want to go back to the youth centre and stare at her bottom,' Kirsty smirked.

I shrugged my shoulders. 'If that's what I've got to suffer through to find out the truth.'

She suddenly giggled. 'OK, Dr Watson, we'll go back and speak to Lynn.'

Dr Watson indeed! 'Sherlock Holmes to you!' I shouted after her.

Our friends had already eaten by the time we got to the Hamburger Palace.

Paul and Gemma seemed to be getting on like a house on fire, but Ash was pretending to be sick into Leanne's Coke and she had a hold of his head and was bashing it against the table.

'I don't think you're allowed to murder people in here,' I said.

Leanne didn't even stop. 'Only human beings,' she said, giving Ash's head another bang. 'He doesn't qualify.'

Ash pulled himself free. 'What time are you taking her back to the zoo?' he asked Kirsty.

She was astounded. 'That's my best friend.'

'You must belong in a zoo as well then,' Ash said, and with that Kirsty rammed a handful of cold chips into Ash's mouth.

'Help!' he shouted. 'I'm being attacked here. Help me, Jamesie.'

So I did. I started to tickle Kirsty and she screamed at the top of her voice. Ash started to tickle Leanne and she did the same. Not wanting to be left out, Paul tickled Gemma. We caused such a commotion that we ended up being thrown out of the place. It was the best fun I'd had in ages.

My mother was waiting at the door of the precinct as we all came rushing towards her. She probably hadn't even left the precinct car park. I could imagine her sitting there, nervously counting down the minutes till it was time to come and get me.

Her face lit up when she saw me, safe and sound, and I was sure there were tears in her eyes as she realised that Paul and Ash were with me too.

'Have you all been together? That's wonderful.'

Kirsty had put on her sweet little-girl face again as soon as my mother appeared. Phoney as a three-pound coin. Couldn't my mother see through it? But no, she was beaming a smile right back at her.

'We've had a great time, haven't we, Jamesie?'

I saw my mother wince at 'Jamesie', but the smile never wavered.

'And we met my friends and Jamesie's and we're all going to the youth centre next Friday.'

This was all news to me, and to Paul and Ash as well, who looked puzzled.

'Are we?' Ash said.

'So you'll come?' Gemma asked Paul. Paul grinned his answer. I had a feeling these two fancied each other. No! Anything but that.

I turned on Kirsty. 'Do you get paid for how many you recruit?'

Kirsty ignored me. 'What would you do with him, Mrs Gordon? He's a real moan, isn't he?'

She spoke as if she was as old as my mother, or my granny.

***

'She is driving me potty,' I told my mother as we were driving home. She had offered to take Kirsty too, but the girls had decided to go back into the precinct with Leanne, who wanted to get something pierced. I dreaded to think what.

And, of course, driving Kirsty home might have meant revealing her real identity.

'She's like a breath of fresh air,' my mother said as we waved them all off.

'She's more like a whiff of poison gas if you ask me.'

My mother glanced at me with a frown. 'You don't have to see her again if you don't want to,' she said.

'I don't think I've got a choice. I think she's decided to adopt me.'

She laughed when I said that. I hadn't seen her laugh in such a long time. And all because of Kirsty Shearer. Because of her I was actually beginning to do things again. I was even back with Paul and Ash. Maybe she was a life-changing experience.

And did I feel guilty about the lies we were telling my mother?

Not really, I decided. Kirsty was the only one who believed me. The only one who wanted to find out the truth as much as I did.

No, I didn't feel guilty. In fact, I realised that, for the first time in an age, I was really enjoying myself.

Chapter 13

They all arrived in force the next Friday for our visit to the youth centre. Ash and Paul came first, bursting into the house with cries and shouts, almost like the old days. Almost.

My mother was beaming with pleasure at seeing them there. She ushered them into the living-room and immediately produced juice and crisps and fruit on the table for them.

'Have we got to wait for those girls?' Ash moaned. 'That Leanne gets on my nerves. Always having a wobbly about something totally trivial.' He began doing an impression of Leanne finding one of her nails broken. 'This is the end of my world. I can never be seen in public again!' he screamed, sounding so like her that Paul and I couldn't stop laughing.

'Can't we just go on to this youth centre without them?' he was pleading.

'They're coming in the van. Remember, I need a special mode of transport now.' I hadn't meant it to sound pitiful. Could have bitten off my tongue for how it came out.

'Oh, yeah.' Ash looked around the room, trying to avoid embarrassing eye contact with me.

Paul still couldn't see a problem. 'Your mum could run us there. You can get your wheelchair in her car.'

I looked at him as if he was mad. 'I don't want my mother turning up with me. Can you imagine how embarrassing that would be?'

Paul shrugged. 'Just have to wait for the girls then.'

Ash gave him a shove. 'You don't mind. You and that Gemma were getting really cosy the other day. Did you see them, James?'

Paul blushed to his roots. 'I was not.'

'I saw you,' I said, laughing. 'Sitting beside each other, whispering, giggling.'

Now Paul was really offended. 'I was not giggling. Only girls giggle.'

He lifted a cushion and tried to suffocate me with it. Ash joined in, jumping on Paul's back and yelling like a savage. I had my hands round Paul's throat. 'Die, pig, die!' I was shouting.

We were yelling so much we didn't hear the door open and the three girls come in.

'Would you look at this, Mrs Gordon. Boys are so childish, aren't they?'

My mother was laughing, and agreeing with Kirsty. Peeking breathlessly from beneath a cushion, the first thing I noticed was that Leanne had a brand new hairstyle. Even worse than the last. Tufts were standing out all over her head, and each tuft was a different colour.

'That has to be a wig,' I said at once.

She patted the tufts. 'This? This is my real hair. D'you like it?'

Ash guffawed loudly. 'You got a lawyer? Sue the hairdresser, dear.'

Kirsty's hair looked exactly as it always did. As if she had woken up from a nightmare and hadn't combed it. She grinned at me. 'Are you ready to go?'

It was impossible not to notice that Paul and Gemma went right up to each other and started talking and laughing.

Kirsty gave me a shove. 'I think she quite fancies him,' she said. And before I could say a word she added, 'Mind you, he's the nicest-looking out of the three of you.'

'What about me?' I asked. 'I'm nice looking as well. My granny told me.'

'Your granny wears glasses, Jamesie. And they're rose-coloured.' Now she giggled.

'Did you get anything pierced on Saturday?' Ash asked Leanne.

She yanked up her jumper. 'My belly button. Want to see it?'

Ash vaulted over the sofa in shock. 'Aaagghh! You are sick. That is awful.'

'Your mother's a Pakistani. I bet she's got lots of things pierced.'

'That's different. That's my mother,' he said.

As we moved out to the van I was still laughing. I hadn't realised just how much I had missed my two friends. And I promised myself that, no matter what, I wouldn't lose them again.

I saw their faces fall as we pulled to a halt at the youth centre. It didn't look very promising. The building was dark and the windows were boarded up with corrugated iron. I tried to reassure them. 'It's better inside. Honest. It's good.'

'If you say so, James.' Ash looked around at the estate. An iron-grey sky hung over the place and made it look even more forbidding. 'I just wish I'd brought my bodyguard with me.'

'Don't worry,' Kirsty said sweetly. 'Me and the girls will protect you weak boys.'

Ash almost chased her inside the building. We could hear the music pounding as we pushed open the doors. A group of people had gathered round the pool table, watching a game. But the biggest crowd was in the disco. I looked around. There was the boy in the wheelchair again, sitting looking bored.

'Doesn't anybody ever talk to him?' I asked Kirsty.

'I told you. He is the biggest bore you'll ever come across. Do you want to talk to him?'

I wheeled away in annoyance. 'No. You're not going to shove the boys in the wheelchairs together, right?'

Kirsty hauled me back and crouched down beside me. 'Now listen, the minister is going to be here tonight. I'll have to say who you are. I just cannot lie to the minister.'

I looked at her in disbelief. 'You? You can't lie to somebody?'

Just then I caught sight of the lovely Lynn, dancing in the disco. 'Look, Kirsty, there's Lynn,' I said, and I was off in a hurry, this time with Kirsty following in my wake.

I was sure Lynn had seen me and was deliberately ignoring me. Not just ignoring, she was moving further away on the dance floor. Trying to hide herself from me. Now why would she do that? Didn't she want to talk to me? Was she hiding something? Or was I just becoming paranoid about everyone?

Kirsty pushed through the dancers and shouted into Lynn's ear. Lynn looked up and pretended this was the first time she had noticed me. She smiled.

She was gorgeous. I had to admit that.

Kirsty steered her towards me, then motioned us both to follow her out of the disco.

'We've been to see Eric Bethel,' Kirsty said at once.

I watched Lynn swallow nervously. 'And what did he say?'

'What did you expect him to say?' I asked, before Kirsty could get another word in.

Lynn hesitated. She blinked. 'You couldn't believe a word he said anyway,' she said. 'He's a junkie.'

'He said he was expecting Sam to come back for him. Do you think he did?'

Lynn began to look annoyed. 'What is this? The three degrees?' She really was thick. Surely she meant the third degree? 'Why are you so interested in all this? How come you think somebody else was driving?'

She still hadn't figured out who I was. So that meant Eric Bethel hadn't been in touch with her. But she was still hiding something. Still afraid we might find out the truth. But what was the truth? It hadn't been Eric Bethel behind the wheel. Who else could it have been?

'Can you think of anybody else that Sam might have picked up after he left you?'

It seemed to me her face went pale, and I held my breath, waiting for her answer. But it never came.

'Hello, how nice to see a new face.' I turned quickly at the sound of the voice. A young red-headed woman stood before me, smiling.

Kirsty beamed at her. 'This is the minister, James. The Reverend McFarlane. We call her Anne.'

I almost laughed. Here I had been expecting a dour, sour-faced, middle-aged man in a dog collar and, instead, the minister was a young woman with bright eyes, wearing jeans and a sweater. She smiled back.

'We can always rely on our Kirsty to recruit new members. And here, she's brought us three.' She held out her hand to me.

'I'm James,' I said.

She nodded. 'Yes, Mr Blackett said your mother had phoned to check us out before she would let you come. I don't blame her. This isn't exactly the best area in the world. But I like to think we have a little haven in our youth centre.'

'It's good,' I said. 'Cool.'

'Well, you and your friends can maybe muck in and help us. We're always looking for handymen, to help us paint and make things and repair things. I'll go and get Donny and he'll get you sorted. He'll have you organised in no time at all.'

Kirsty smirked. 'Jamesie wouldn't be able to do anything. He couldn't paint to save his life.'

'I beg your pardon,' I argued. 'I've always helped with decorating.' I looked at Anne. 'You tell me what you need done and I'll see to it, Reverend.'

She grinned. 'Just call me Anne.'

As she walked away, I said to Kirsty, 'I like her. She's really nice. I thought she'd be a man.'

'Typical boy. If it's a minister, it's got to be a man. I suppose if it's a nurse it's got to be a woman.' Kirsty stuck out her tongue at me, but I just grinned.

'No, honest, I thought this Donny was the minister.'

'Donny was at the conference with her. He is brilliant. He practically runs this place, and he organises things, and he gets us money for outings and everything. He helped me and my dad so much when our Sam died.'

'You sound as if you're in love,' I said.

'I can think of worse people to fall in love with. I mean, let's face it, Lynn Mitchell is as thick as they come. The three degrees indeed!'

'Why have you always got to start an argument?' I looked around. 'Where's Lynn gone anyway?'

'I know love is blind, James, but I think maybe Lynn didn't want to talk to us. It was obvious to me. I think she's frightened in case she says too much. Now, what could she be so scared of?'

'Maybe she knows who was really driving that night,' I said.

'If it's Eric Bethel, no wonder she's scared.'

'It wasn't Eric Bethel I saw.' Why couldn't she believe that?

Kirsty looked as if she still wasn't convinced. 'Of course it might help if you could describe him better.'

'I'll know him when I see him,' I told her.

And suddenly I did see him. He was coming across the room and he was heading straight for me.

Chapter 14

I began to shake. I was back in the nightmare of the crash, with lights blinding me, with the rain and terror. And that face rushing towards me.

I gripped Kirsty's hand, tried to tell her, but the words wouldn't come.

It was as if my world had gone into slow motion. There were no sounds, except for my own heart beating faster. The man seemed to float towards me, his soft, fair hair flopping against his forehead, his eyes never leaving me. And I was afraid.

He came forward, smiling, and crouched down in front of me. 'Hi,' he said, holding out his hand. 'I'm Donny Scanlon.'

This wasn't what I had been expecting. No wonder I was in shock. This was the man who ran the youth centre, who organised it. Kirsty thought he was brilliant. Yet, without doubt, this was the man I had seen in the hospital. The same man who had been driving the van on the night of the crash.

Kirsty almost jumped on him and gave him a hug. 'Hiya, Donny. We've missed you here.'

He gave her a playful punch on the chin. 'I've missed you too, Kirsty.'

Anne came up, smiling, and heard the last words. 'You're going to miss him even more, aren't they, Donny?' she said. 'Donny's got that job in America. Great opportunity for him.'

Kirsty looked disappointed. 'Really? Oh no, what are you going to do without me, Donny?'

'I think he might survive, Kirsty.' Anne turned her attention on me. 'Have you met our James, Donny?' For the first time someone noticed how white I must have looked. 'Are you all right, James?'

'You're white as a sheet, Jamesie. Are you OK?' Kirsty bent down to me, her face full of concern.

My mouth was so dry my lips were stuck together. I could hardly speak. I couldn't take my eyes off Donny Scanlon's smiling face.

Kirsty was grinning at him. Even the minister was smiling with nothing but admiration. Well, I didn't care.

I wasn't going to let him get away with it. I had found him, at last. And everybody was going to know it.

'It was you,' I said, breathlessly.

Donny Scanlon looked puzzled. 'Me?'

'Don't pretend you don't know what I'm talking about. My name's James Gordon, and it's because of you I'm in this wheelchair. You were driving the van that ran into my dad's car. You!' I was growing angrier as I spoke. My voice was getting louder. 'I saw you. I remember. I've been looking for you. That's why I'm here. And I've found you and I won't let you get away with it. I'm going to get the police on to you. You're going to jail.'

'What is all this about? Who exactly are you?' Anne asked, still puzzled.

I didn't take my eyes off Donny Scanlon's face. 'Ask him – bet he remembers. James Gordon. He killed my dad that night as well. And he let Kirsty's brother take the blame.'

There was a gasp from Anne at that. For the first time she had realised what I was talking about, realised exactly who I was.

I was drawing a crowd. People had stopped playing table tennis, were looking over at us. Stepping over from the pinball machines and the pool tables to see what all the commotion was about. Even Paul and Ash and the girls were moving closer.

Donny Scanlon was too dumbfounded to say a word. But his face had gone as white as chalk.

'What do you know about this, Kirsty?' Anne demanded angrily.

For the first time since I'd known her, Kirsty sounded apprehensive. 'James told me it wasn't our Sam driving that night. I wanted that to be true, Anne. Honest. I brought him here because I thought we might find something out. Somebody else *was* driving that night. I know it. But I didn't realise he was going to blame Donny.'

I turned on her angrily. 'Donny *is* to blame. Don't you believe me?'

'You're mistaken, son,' Donny Scanlon said softly.

Anne touched his arm reassuringly. 'Of course he is, Donny.' She looked at Kirsty. 'You had no right to do this, Kirsty. And as for you, James, I think you'd better leave. I'll get the van.'

'I don't want the van!' I yelled out. I was even angrier now. 'I want the police. Are you not listening to what I'm saying?'

The music in the disco screeched off, and there was silence, silence except for me.

They were all watching me, some puzzled, some annoyed, but none of them looking as if they believed a word I was saying. I turned to Kirsty. 'You've got to believe me. It was him.'

But even Kirsty, super-confident Kirsty, bit her lip and shook her head. 'But how, Jamesie? Donny wasn't even with Sam that night.'

'Says who, Kirsty?'

'If I need an alibi, I'm sure I've got one.' Donny Scanlon smiled, the only one who did smile. He smiled in that patronising way I had grown to hate. Keep the boy in the wheelchair happy – he has enough problems.

'You'll need one OK. It better be a good one. Because I'm an eyewitness.'

The Reverend Anne's voice was cold. 'So why haven't you come forward before, James?'

And I know the answer to that was weak and sounded silly. 'Because I couldn't remember. But I saw him at the hospital and as soon as I saw his face, I remembered. He was the one who was driving the van.'

Already Anne was shaking her head. 'Sam Shearer was the only one in the van that night. I won't have you blaming an innocent man. If you say things like that, it could lead to a lot of trouble for you.'

Donny Scanlon was all understanding. 'No, it won't, James. I understand. You're mixed up, you're emotional. It's understandable.'

I looked around at all the faces. Not one of them understood or believed me. They looked at me with pity, and I hated that. Not even Kirsty looked as if she believed me any more. That only made me more frustrated. 'Don't you talk to me as if I'm stupid. I'm right. And I won't let you get away with it.'

Anne stood up straight. 'Right, that's it. You're going home, James.'

'Why doesn't anyone believe me?' I yelled. 'Because I'm in a wheelchair? I'm not daft as well, you know.'

Paul and Ash came forward and tried to calm me down, but I shrugged them off. If causing a scene was the only way I was going to get anyone to listen to me, then I would. 'I want somebody to call the police. I want him arrested!'

But in the end it wasn't the police who were called. It was my mother.

Chapter 15

I lay slumped on my bed watching some stupid children's TV presenter jumping around trying to look cool. Watching TV was all I had done since the night at the centre when my mother had brought me home.

I hadn't felt like this since just after the accident. So low, so depressed. I was useless. I knew the truth, but no one would believe me. Not even Kirsty.

And the humiliation I had felt when my mother arrived at the centre would never leave me either. I was still yelling at the top of my voice, accusing Donny Scanlon. No one could shut me up. Anne had tried to get me into the office to quieten me down but I had clung on to a pillar and refused to move. By the time my mother came they were all sure I was hysterical. I wasn't. I just wanted someone to believe me.

And all the while Donny Scanlon couldn't have been nicer. As soon as my mother came into the hall, he went forward to her and held out his hand.

'My name's Donny Scanlon, and it seems I'm the cause of all this.'

And my mother had taken his hand and actually smiled at him.

That was just too much. I had rammed my wheelchair against Scanlon's legs, and my mother had let out a scream.

'James! Enough of this!'

'But, Mum, he's—'

She wouldn't let me go on. Wouldn't listen. She even started to apologise for me. That made me even angrier. Anne tried to explain what had happened and as she did I watched my mum's face grow whiter. Her eyes turned to Kirsty as she was told her true identity at last.

'You little liar,' she said. 'You came into my house and you deliberately lied to me.'

Kirsty jumped forward. 'But, Mrs Gordon, James phoned my house, he told me my brother wasn't to blame for the accident. I had to come. And I couldn't tell you who I was.'

'Your brother *was* to blame. There was no one else in that van, and James and you will just have to accept that.'

'I won't! I won't!' I yelled at the top of my voice. I was annoying people. I could see that. Ash and Paul on either side of me were trying to calm me down, but I wouldn't be calmed.

And all the while Donny Scanlon smiled.

'I'll get you! You wait and see if I don't,' I shouted at him.

Donny Scanlon turned to my mother. 'He's upset. Please don't blame him for this.'

And the hardest thing was that they were all towering above me, talking over me, apologising for me. No wonder I was angry. Angry and humiliated. I was still yelling as my mother pushed my wheelchair out into the courtyard to her car.

They all came to the door to watch me go. Ash and Paul had wanted to come home with me, but my mother had declined that offer. But then so had I. I hadn't wanted them there. I never wanted to see anyone again. I had watched as they all became tiny figures in the distance, standing at the doors of the centre.

I had expected a screaming match with my mother when we got home, but that hadn't materialised. Instead, all she'd said to me when we had arrived home that night was, 'I can't take any more of this, James.'

If I had gone into a depression, so had she. She made my meals. She washed, she ironed, she shopped. But she hardly spoke to me.

She couldn't take any more if it? That was a laugh. What did she have to suffer? She was alive. She wasn't in a wheelchair. And, even worse, she had treated me like an idiot. An idiot who couldn't be believed.

Paul and Ash called, but I refused to see them. They hadn't believed me either. Ash had even tried to joke that I'd only had a 'wobbly', just like Leanne. Some wobbly, I thought.

And Kirsty? Kirsty would never be allowed in the house again. My mother had made that clear on the way home in her car. Babbling on about lying girls, and people who couldn't be trusted. 'How dare she?' she kept repeating. But then, I didn't want to see her either. I had expected that at least she would believe me, but she hadn't. Eric Bethel was the one she had wanted to be guilty, not Donny Scanlon. He was something special. Everyone thought so. No one was ever going to believe he was guilty of anything.

I felt as if I was falling down a black hole and I knew the further down I went, the harder it would be for me to climb up again.

I wouldn't have got any sympathy from Kirsty, I thought. She would have been shouting at me. Yelling at me. Refusing to let me feel sorry for myself.

I'd only known her for a couple of weeks and yet in those weeks she'd infuriated me, made me laugh, made me feel alive. I'd looked forward to each day with Kirsty. With her, my brain was constantly working, planning, thinking. I had enjoyed those days when Ash and Paul had come back into my life, and that was thanks to Kirsty as well.

Now I was back to what I had been before I met her. Hating my life, my mother, hating everything. I had never been so miserable.

Chapter 16

It was Kirsty I was thinking about when my mobile phone began to ring. Paul again, maybe, I thought, or Ash. Usually I just didn't answer, but this time I didn't recognise the number which came up.

'Hello?' I asked into the phone.

'It's me, Jamesie.' Kirsty. Her voice unusually soft. 'Is your mum there? Switch off if she is. Say it was a wrong number. She'll go spare if she finds out I'm phoning you.'

'Why *are* you phoning me?' I asked. Not that I cared. Nothing mattered any more.

'I still believe you, Jamesie,' she said at once.

'Took your time, didn't you? You might have stuck up for me at the centre.'

'I don't mean I think it was Donny. He could never do anything like that. He would never let someone else take the blame, especially my brother. But I've had time to think about it. They kind of look alike, same hair . . . Eric Bethel and Donny, maybe . . .'

I almost hung up on her. 'I'm not interested if you don't believe it was Donny Scanlon.'

She shouted, 'Listen to me! We've still got to work together. Right. I believe somebody else was driving. I think it was Eric or one of his cronies, maybe. You think it was Donny. Either way, we still want to find out the truth. Right. And we're better doing it together. I just need to know it wasn't my brother.'

'It makes no difference,' I said. 'No one's going to believe anything I say now.'

'So you're just going to let him get away with it.'

'He already has.'

'Only if you let him.' She suddenly got angry. 'Jamesie! What is wrong with you?'

'I'm useless. That's what wrong with me.'

There was a long sigh on the line. For a second I thought she'd hung up on me. Not Kirsty. She launched into an angry tirade. 'Useless, are you? 'Cause you're in a wheelchair? 'Cause your legs don't work? Your brain still works, doesn't it? You make me sick, James Gordon. You're always feeling sorry for yourself. You can't walk. Big deal. You're *alive*. Your dad's *dead*. My brother's *dead*. But oh no, you're the unlucky one. You're the one everybody's to feel sorry for. Well, you're right, Jamesie. In fact, you're not just useless. You're pathetic.'

And she was gone.

I threw the phone at the wall with such force it bounced back and hit the desk with a crack. How dare she talk to me like that? I didn't want people to feel sorry for me. I was glad I was alive. What a cheek she had, saying those things. I hated her.

My mother came rushing into the room. 'What was that noise?' She must have seen the anger in my face. 'Is everything OK?'

'No, everything's not OK,' I said. I was breathing heavily, angrier than I'd been in ages. My mother was almost out of the room before I spoke again. 'I've had a lot of time to think, and I want my mates back here. Paul and Ash.'

I saw her face crease into a relieved smile. She began nodding. 'I'm so glad.'

'I felt better when I had them back.' And I had. I had promised myself never to lose them again, and I wouldn't. No matter what. 'But I want something else too.'

I knew she wouldn't smile when I said this. 'I want Kirsty Shearer here as well.'

'No!' she said at once. 'I will not have that little liar in my house again.'

'Yeah, she is a liar. I know. And she's annoying and she drives me potty, but you know what I've just figured out, Mum? She treated me the way she treats everybody else. As if I'm normal. She doesn't make any allowances for me. She doesn't feel sorry for me. In fact, I don't even think she likes me very much. But you know what? She sees *me*, not my wheelchair. She treats me the way I want to be treated, and I want her to come back. Please, Mum.'

Mum didn't say anything for a moment. She sat down on the sofa, and I was afraid she was about to cry again.

Instead, she looked up at me, and her expression had changed. There were no tears in her eyes. She looked stern. 'So, that's what you want, James? No allowances made, eh? Somebody to see you and not your wheelchair?' She didn't wait for an answer. She didn't really want any. She stood up and began striding about the room. 'Well, that's fine by me. For months I've been pussyfooting around you. Trying to make up for what happened. Feeling guilty. I left my job to teach you at home. My whole life's been on hold, caring for you. Worrying about you. Trying to please you. And now I find what I should have been doing all the time was insulting you. Arguing with you. Not letting you off with anything.' She bent right down and snapped out the words into my face. 'From now on, I won't. Gone is sad, crying little mother. Blaming herself for everything. She is gone forever, James. Here to stay is me. The mother from hell. The mother who won't let you get away with a thing from now on.'

I shrank back from her. She was scary like this.

'You want your lying little friend back. Fine. I'll get her back. But I'll tell you this, boy, from now on things are going to change around here.'

Chapter 17

How things could change in just a few days. One minute the house was empty and quiet and dull, and the next there was an explosion of noise and activity and music. Paul and Ash arrived later that week, bustling in through the door, expecting to have to cheer me up. Instead they found me anxious to see them, laughing and smiling.

'Everything all right after the other . . . eh . . . night?'

I grinned. 'Sorry about that. Won't happen again.'

Paul zapped me on the shoulder. 'Don't worry about it. Did you really think that Donny was—?'

I didn't let him finish. 'I did. I was sure I'd seen him before and it was at the wheel of that car. But I must have been mistaken, eh?'

'Your mother says you've been through such a lot, it's bound to have got you all mixed up?' It was more of a question, as if Ash didn't quite believe that.

Paul grinned. 'It's a pity, though. You've blown going back there. It was a good centre. Good place to go.'

Ash laughed. 'You only want to go back to see Gemma!'

Paul jumped on him and they started fighting. 'Take that back!'

I had already thought about going back to the centre. It was almost all I had thought about. 'Don't you think they'd let me?'

Ash laughed. 'You? Hannibal Lecter's got a better chance of getting back in there.'

Paul was puzzled. 'Would you want to go back? Wouldn't Donny always remind you of your . . .?'

'I made a mistake about Donny Scanlon.' I found it easy to say his name. 'I really think I should go back and apologise to him. Tell him I was wrong.'

I would've loved to have told them the truth, that I was still convinced Donny Scanlon was to blame, but I had decided the fewer people who knew the better.

The boys hadn't been in the house for long when the doorbell rang again. This time it was Kirsty, flanked for safety by Leanne and Gemma.

Ash groaned. 'You didn't tell us they'd be coming.'

Leanne made a face. 'It must be your lucky day then.'

My mother was with them, leading them into my room with hardly a glance at Kirsty. Pretending she wasn't there.

Her smiles, such as they were, she kept for the boys. The door had snapped shut behind her before Kirsty even dared to open her mouth. 'I was dead scared there. I thought she was going to shout and bawl at me.' She gave one of her dramatic sighs. 'That's why I brought Leanne and Gemma. Protection.'

Already the girls were rifling through my CD collection. 'Put this on, James.' Leanne held up one of them. 'I want to show Kirsty and Gemma the dance that goes with it.'

Ash swiped the CD from her. 'What do you think this is? *Top of the Pops*? We're not going to have a daft dancing lesson from you.'

Leanne jumped for the CD. 'Give me that back.'

But Ash had already thrown it to Paul. 'Catch!' Paul did, and this time it was Gemma who dived for the CD.

'Watch that!' I shouted, but I was already laughing and when the CD flew my way I caught it deftly and flicked it back to Ash. By this time Kirsty had joined in.

'Right, whoever gets it decides what to do. If the girls get it, you've got to learn the dance as well. Right?'

The boys agreed readily. After all, whoever heard of girls winning in a catching contest?

So that was why when my mother came in half an hour later Paul and Ash were in a line with the girls trying to dance.

She looked amused at first, then alarmed. Afraid the sight of dancing would remind me that I never would dance. She glanced at me and seemed amazed that I was laughing too. 'Have you ever seen anything so funny in your life?' I called to her above the din. 'And I don't have to do it. Sometimes being in this wheelchair's got its good side.'

She looked even more amazed and, to be honest, so was I. A good side to being here? I had never thought I would say that. Even in a joke. But it was true. I might turn the wheels around in time to the music, but I didn't have to make the complete fool of myself that my two pals were making.

'I'm popping across to Mrs McIntosh,' my mother said, and that took me by surprise. She never left me alone. 'If you want anything to eat, you can help yourself in the kitchen.'

Then she went. As soon as she did, Kirsty stopped dancing and came and sat beside me. 'How did you get her to change her mind about me?'

'I don't think I did. A lot of things have changed, Kirsty. The way she's been treating me over the past few days. Different. Like now, leaving us alone, telling me to help myself in the kitchen ... and do you know what?' I grinned at her. 'I like it.'

'I had to tell my dad about you. Anne made me. I had to ask permission to come back here and see you.' Kirsty couldn't look at me now.

'He knows you're here with me? He doesn't mind?'

'No. He doesn't mind. As long as I'm enjoying myself.' She squeezed my arm. 'You're going to come back to the centre, aren't you, Jamesie?'

'What makes you think I should go back?'

'Because if you got to know Donny, you'd realise he could never do that. He just couldn't.'

I nodded. 'I'm going to come back, Kirsty, if they'll let me. But I'm doing it to prove to you that, no matter what you think, Donny Scanlon was the driver that night. And I'm not going to let him get away with it.'

Chapter 18

'You want to go back to the youth centre?' My mother was more than surprised. She was alarmed. 'No. I don't think that's a good idea.'

I wasn't going to let this go. 'Just the once, Mum. I want to apologise to Donny. I made such a fool of myself. Paul and Ash say they'll come with me. I've asked them.'

'I don't think Donny Scanlon will want you there, apology or not. You caused quite a scene. The things you said to him.'

I had an answer for that one. 'He's supposed to be a really nice guy, Mum. I'm sure he'll let me come. You saw how understanding he was that night. He never even broke sweat and I was hurling abuse at him.' I held up my hands. 'But if he doesn't want me to, end of story.'

'I suppose it would be nice if you apologised.' She hesitated. 'You realise now you made a terrible mistake? You couldn't have seen anyone at the wheel of that car.'

'It was the dream, Mum, and then seeing him at the hospital right after. And then when I saw him coming towards me at the centre . . . I just got mixed up.' I must have convinced her for she went off to phone Anne and I listened as she asked, and knew from what Mum was saying that Anne had the same concerns she had. But how could Donny Scanlon refuse? The boy in the wheelchair wanted to apologise. How could such a paragon of virtue turn down that offer? And by the time Mum came back into the living-room I knew he hadn't.

'Anne got him on his mobile phone. He is a nice fellow, James. Reluctantly,' she stressed that, '*very* reluctantly, he'll be glad to see you at the centre on Friday.'

Yes, I thought. Very reluctantly. He hadn't wanted me to go back, not now that he realised I knew the truth. But he couldn't very well refuse. It wouldn't have done his 'nice guy' image much good.

Mum sat down beside me and took my hands in hers. 'James, this has to be the end of this crazy notion you've got that you saw who was driving that night. We know who was driving, and he's dead. I'm glad to see you getting on with your life – you don't know how glad – though I'd rather it was as far away from that Kirsty as possible. I'm willing to let that pass, she does seem good for you. But, James, you've got to promise me, no more scenes. I've had enough.'

I squeezed her hand back. 'No more scenes, Mum.' I didn't feel guilty. I didn't even blush as I said it. No more scenes, and I meant that. I was planning, instead, to be the best actor in the world. Pretending I'd made a mistake. Why, I would even pretend I was getting to like Donny as much as everyone else. Because, if the only way I was going to get Donny Scanlon was by watching him and getting to know him, I would. Sooner or later, his guard would drop and he'd give himself away.

It seemed I couldn't get rid of Paul and Ash those next few days. It was great having them back. I'd almost forgotten how much they could make me laugh. We played on the computer and the PlayStation. We talked about football. It still hurt when they told me all about their latest game, but not so much.

'This is great,' Ash said as we munched sandwiches. 'I thought we'd never be able to come back here like this.'

'It's thanks to Kirsty,' Paul said.

I groaned. 'It is not. It's time. Time makes things better. Not good. Don't think I feel better about being in here.' I patted the chair. 'I'll always hate this. But I hated having no mates even more.'

Ash put on one of his silly voices. 'Oh, he missed us, Paul.'

'I missed you like the plague,' I shouted at him.

'I still think you've got Kirsty to thank.'

Paul was right. I knew that. But I wasn't going to admit it, especially to Paul. I had a feeling he would pass the word to Gemma, and then it would go straight to Kirsty. And she wasn't getting the credit for anything.

Her dad was lying on the sofa in a drunken sleep. Kirsty decided it was a good time to ask him. She had told James that her dad didn't mind what she did. And that was almost true. The real truth was, he didn't care. But she always asked anyway.

'That boy, that James Gordon, the one I told you about? He's going back to the youth centre. Is it all right if I go back too? Anne says I can go back if you agree. It might seem funny, the two of us becoming friends, but, really, it's the Christian thing to do, Dad. Fate brought us together. He's lost somebody and I've lost somebody, and together we can be a support and comfort for each other.'

It was practically word for word what she'd said to Anne when she asked about coming back with James. And it was practically word for word what she'd heard in an American TV film a few days ago.

Her dad couldn't hear her. He lifted a droopy eyelid, but he didn't actually see her either. He wouldn't care if I left now and never came back, Kirsty thought bitterly. She brushed a strand of hair back from his face.

'So you don't mind, then, if I go back there with him?'

He let out a snore in answer. Sounded like a 'yes' to her.

So she could go now with a clear conscience. She had to find out the truth.

But what was the truth? She believed James had seen someone else that night. But, of course, it couldn't have been Donny. Donny was the nicest person she had ever come across. He had helped both her and her dad so much after Sam had died. A shoulder to cry on, someone to talk to. And if James came back to the centre and saw how much Donny did for everyone there, he'd realise what a mistake he had made. No. If anyone else was driving, surely it had to be Eric Bethel. And together she and James were going to prove it.

Chapter 19

My mum insisted on coming with me that first night back at the youth centre. I would have preferred her not to come, but there was no point in arguing. If anything, she was more nervous than I was. And I was nervous. I had made a complete fool of myself the last time I was there. It was going to be hard going back amongst all those people again. But not as hard as facing Donny Scanlon.

I hated him, knew without doubt he was the face I had seen that night, yet here I was, going back to actually apologise for accusing him. But I didn't know what else to do. I had to find out the truth. I had to keep watching him.

We didn't wait for the van that night. Mum took me in the car. And we didn't wait for Kirsty either. In spite of several visits from the girls, Mum would hardly look at her. Paul and Ash were different. She trusted them completely, daft as brushes though both of them were. They came with us in the car and their laughing and their jokes took my mind off what was ahead.

There didn't seem to be so many people at the centre that night. Had they heard I was coming? Mad boy in a wheelchair? There was a couple playing at the pool table. Two boys lingered at the pinball machines. The disco looked sparse and even the music was dismal. I moved inside with Mum beside me.

Ash put a hand on my shoulder. 'We're right here, boyo,' he said.

The Reverend Anne appeared from the office. She caught sight of us and waved us towards her. This was it and I wasn't looking forward to it.

I wished Kirsty was with me, but there was no sign of her or her friends.

When we went into the office, Scanlon looked uncomfortable. He didn't want me here, but couldn't actually say why. He'd had no choice but to agree to welcome me. I was apologising. Admitting how wrong I had been. It's amazing what you can get away with when you're in a wheelchair.

Could he see in my eyes that I still didn't trust him? I looked at him, and shivered. The memory of that night came rushing back to me like a derailed express train. Could he see that? If he did, he was a good actor. He smiled. He stepped forward and held out his hand.

'You're sure this is what you want, James?'

I stared at him, and my hand was like lead as I raised it to his. His touch was cold and clammy. Nerves. But then, I was nervous too.

'I'm . . . sorry . . . I shouldn't have said what I did. I made a terrible mistake.'

Donny Scanlon shook his head. 'No, James. That's apology enough. You don't have to say anything else. Your mum's explained about you seeing me at the hospital.' He leaned forward. 'It took a lot of guts to come back and do this.'

He thought it was over, that I was going to leave now and he'd never have to see me again.

I swallowed. 'But . . . actually, I want to keep coming back . . . if that's OK with you.'

I could see I had taken him by surprise. One visit, one apology he could handle. But me there week after week – now that would be a different story.

I had taken my mother by surprise too. I hadn't told her that was my plan. 'Oh no, James. I don't think that would be a good idea.'

But I had an answer for her all ready. 'Mum, this is the first place I've been able to come to and have fun. It's good here, you said so yourself. And Ash and Paul want to come back too. I won't cause any more trouble.' I tried to put on a 'Kirsty'-type look. Innocent and totally believable.

It must have worked. 'I think we should leave that decision to Donny,' Anne said. 'It's entirely up to you, Donny,' she smiled at him. 'You're the one he insulted.'

Now she turned her attention to me. 'But we can't have you here if you aren't sincere about this apology.'

I looked up at Donny. 'Of course I am.'

Donny Scanlon's eyes never left mine. He knew what I was saying. I still knew he was guilty. But I knew too he could never say he didn't want me here. Not if he had nothing to feel guilty about.

He forced a smile. 'How can I say no?'

How, indeed, Donny boy, I thought.

Donny tried to sound relaxed. He didn't fool me. 'I'm not surprised you want to come back, James. We've got a good centre here.' He glanced at Anne. 'Isn't that right?'

Anne agreed. 'Thanks to you, Donny,' she said. She looked at Mum. 'Donny is responsible for how good this place is. His work with young people has drawn so many away from the drugs and the crime in this area. When I first started this centre, it was hard getting people to come. Especially since it was run by a minister, and a woman.' She looked fondly at Donny. 'But then Donny got involved. He brought in so many good ideas, ideas that kept the young people coming in.'

They all thought he was a hero. That was obvious. He couldn't be a villain. I was going to have a really hard time proving otherwise.

Donny moved off to see to some problem or other with the games machines. Anne looked after him with affection. 'I don't know what we'll do without him. He works so hard for this centre. For young people here. He always has. Now he's got a wonderful chance with this new job in America, working with young people in a summer camp. Disabled young people,' she added significantly.

I knew this was meant for me, to prove to me how wonderful Donny Scanlon was. Only I knew the kind of person he really was.

My mum left shortly afterwards, assured by Anne that the van would take me home and that Paul and Ash would accompany me in it.

'Feel better now it's done?' she asked before she left.

I dodged the question. 'Had to do it, didn't I?'

She looked around the bustling hall. It was already filling up. 'You know I've said to Anne I'd like to come along here and help too. It's a really good project. And it's on three nights a week for different age groups. Would you mind if I did that?' I was never going to get away from her. She was going to follow me for the rest of my life. But the old pity I used to be able to force on to her had gone forever. 'I'm coming anyway. I'm a teacher. I'm good with young people. They need trained people here with ideas. So stick that up your wheelchair!'

I was smiling when she left, and Paul came up to me and asked why.

'I've just been told off by my mum,' I said, leaving him totally puzzled.

I saw Leanne and Gemma prancing in through the door then, but no Kirsty. Leanne was having another of her 'wobblies'.

'What on earth's wrong with you?' Ash asked as she danced and jumped about and screeched. 'You look as if you've got itching powder in your knickers.'

She gave him a shove. 'Worse than that – my belly button's festering.'

Ash looked totally disgusted. 'Festering?'

Leanne began to explain to him as if he was stupid. 'You know, it's gone all gooey and green and sticky. It's gone bad.'

'I know what festering means. I just think it sounds revolting.'

Paul and Ash both looked as if they were about to be sick.

Leanne must have thought that was a compliment. 'Do you want to see it?'

'No, I do not want to see it! You are the sickest female I've ever come across.'

'Where's Kirsty?' I asked Gemma. 'I thought she might have turned up.'

Gemma blew a bubble. 'She says she'll be along later. I hope her old dad's not drunk again. Poor Kirsty, she always seems to be looking after him.'

I was puzzled. 'She never told me that.'

Gemma shrugged. 'She doesn't tell anyone. He's always been a drinker, but he's been worse since Sam died. Kirsty mollycoddles him. She looks after him as if he was a baby.'

'Yeah,' Leanne agreed. 'My dad says he needs a good kick up the—'

'Right, less of the language,' Ash said, 'or the Reverend Anne'll throw us out.'

Kirsty's dad, a drunk. How many people's lives had been ruined by what had happened that night?

I watched Donny Scanlon move around the hall, smiling and laughing. Except his, I thought. His life was just getting better and better. And I knew then that I had to find a way to prove his guilt before he went off to America.

Chapter 20

In the next two weeks I watched constantly for that dark side of Donny Scanlon. I don't know what I expected to see. Would he suddenly whip off his mask and become a heartless villain? Would he try to electrocute everyone with the disco equipment? Was he a secret assassin for a terror network? Covering up all his nastiness by being Mr Wonderful at the youth centre?

And yet Donny Scanlon just seemed to get nicer and nicer. It was hard not to grow to like him. He fixed machines that were broken, and took the time and the patience to let one of the slowest boys who came to the centre help him. He picked people up when they needed a lift. He took them home. Nothing was too much trouble. He had even learned sign language so he could communicate with one of the boys who was deaf. No wonder they thought so much of him.

But he watched me. I could feel him sometimes, as I wheeled myself around, feel his eyes piercing into me. When I would look over and catch him, he always smiled.

'Enjoying yourself?' he would ask, and I would always reply, because it was true, 'Yeah, it's great.'

'You must see he could never have been driving and let our Sam take the blame,' Kirsty said, over and over. 'It would take a really horrible person to do that, and he's not.'

I had thought I would watch him and eventually he would let slip the real side of him, the nasty side. Instead, everything I saw only made me think that here was a really nice young man. There didn't seem to be a dark side, and yet I knew – only I knew – that there was. He *had* been driving that night, he had killed my dad and he had walked off and let Sam Shearer take the blame. I just couldn't understand how such a nice guy could do that.

One night, I saw him walk towards the other boy in the wheelchair. Peter. Peter always annoyed me. He would sit slumped in the corner and when anyone would try to strike up a conversation with him, he would turn away and ignore them, or else he would talk nothing but nonsense, so in the end people just moved away. I never bothered with him, convinced he was one sandwich short of a picnic.

'Come on, Peter,' Donny called out to him. 'I'm going to need help with putting the chairs away. Come and help me.'

I had seen him trying to get Peter involved before.

Peter, slack-jawed, just gawped at him. 'Me?' he asked. His tone was surly.

Donny nodded at him. 'Yes, you. We'll get the chairs away and then you can help me with the disco equipment.'

'I'm waiting for the van,' he said sourly.

'Well, while you're waiting for the van you can help me.'

He said it sharply, but I knew what he was trying to do. He was trying to make Peter realise that he wasn't helpless. That he could be just as much help as anybody else. Reluctantly, Peter moved forward. He pulled one of the chairs and dragged it against the wall.

'That's the boy, Peter,' Donny said, almost ignoring him. As if it wasn't important what he was doing. But I could see. Donny Scanlon was trying to treat him just the way he would treat any other able-bodied boy who came to the centre.

Out of the corner of my eye, I watched as Peter helped stack chairs against the wall, and then Donny ordered him into the disco to dismantle the equipment there.

'Isn't your brother a DJ, Peter?' Donny asked him as he wound flex around his hand.

Peter nodded. 'Plays at weddings, an' that,' he said sullenly.

'Well, you must know plenty about this stuff. You could probably do a bit of DJing yourself. Couldn't you? Get a few tips from your brother?'

I saw, for the very first time, Peter's eyes light up.

'That's just what the disco needs. A DJ. But we can't afford to pay one. How about it, Peter?'

Peter's shoulders slumped. 'I probably wouldn't be able to do it any good. I'd be rubbish.'

Donny threw out that notion. 'You'd learn. Your brother would help you. Give it a try, eh? Maybe next week?'

Peter shrugged as if he wasn't much interested. But I could see he was. Just for a second, he had come to life. Thanks to Donny Scanlon.

And he was going to work with people just like Peter in America. People just like me. He would be good with them.

What was I thinking? That it would be better if Donny Scanlon was allowed to get on with his life? I had thought coming to the centre would make me more determined to get him. I wanted to keep on hating him. Yet I just seemed to be getting more mixed up.

Donny glanced over at me. Knew I was watching him. Had it all been done for my benefit? I thought, partly, it had been. But only partly.

'Got to get everybody helping out here, James,' he said. 'It's not a charity.'

I knew my presence made him nervous. Knew he was always trying to impress me. How did he stand it, I wondered, knowing I knew the truth?

'How long have you been doing this?' I asked him, after Peter had gone home. He always went off first in the van because he lived in the opposite direction to me.

'I came here as a teenager. Not much older than you. If I hadn't, I might have gone the way of Eric Bethel or . . .'

'Sam Shearer?' I said.

He shrugged his answer.

'This area needed something like this, James. Too many of the young people were hanging about street corners, getting in with the wrong crowd.' He was trying to convince me what a good job he was doing. 'I just love working with young people, James. I've always felt I had a lot to offer.' He sat down beside me so his eyes were on a level with mine.

'When does your job in America start?'

He smiled. 'I'll be leaving here in a couple of weeks.'

My heart started racing. That's why he had agreed to my coming back here. In a couple of weeks he would be gone. Safe. A couple of weeks. Was that what he was asking? Just give me a couple of weeks? And then I'll go and never bother you again. Or was I the one who was considering it?

'This job in America. You don't know how much it means to me. It's a wonderful chance. I can help so many youngsters.' His voice was sincere. His eyes intent on me. He was trying to tell me that, no matter what I knew, I couldn't tell on him. He had too much to lose.

'You mean you can't afford to get into any trouble or you'll lose the job?' I waited for his reaction.

He was breathing hard. 'I've never been in any trouble, James. You have to believe that.' He hesitated. For a moment I thought the conversation was over. That he was about to stand up and move off. But he didn't. His hand clenched nervously on the arm of my chair. 'You know, James. This new job, they offer trips of a lifetime for disabled youngsters. All expenses paid. I could probably get you one. You'd love to go to America, wouldn't you? What do you think about that?'

He almost had me feeling sorry for him, until that moment.

'Are you trying to bribe me, Donny?'

His eyes blinked nervously and, for the first time, for just a split second, he looked angry. 'What would I have to bribe you for?'

He knew that as well as I did.

Just then Anne appeared. Donny stood up. He smiled at the reverend. The 'wonderful guy' kind of smile. 'Just telling James here about my new job.'

'And you're going to be so good at it.'

She patted his shoulder. Donny grinned at me and walked off. But just for an instant I had seen that other side of Donny Scanlon. He was afraid. Afraid because I had it in my power to ruin his chances. And when you're afraid you can get desperate. I shivered. At that moment, I was afraid too.

Chapter 21

'What's wrong with your face?' Kirsty asked me. We were enjoying our usual Saturday afternoon visit to the precinct. Yes. Enjoying. I looked forward to so many of my days now. But that Saturday I was thoughtful. My mind was taken up with Donny Scanlon. I was obsessed with him. One minute he was someone it was hard not to like. The next, I was afraid of him. Since talking to him last night, I was even more mixed up about how I really felt about him.

I told Kirsty what he had said to me. She wasn't convinced it could have been a bribe of any kind. 'I've told you, Jamesie, he is SO nice. I've never known him to do a bad thing in my life.'

Nothing was going to change her mind. She already had her villain.

Leanne suddenly yelped. 'Who says we all go to the pictures tonight? There's a dead romantic film on I'm dying to see.'

Ash and Paul groaned.

'I am not going to any romantic picture,' Ash told her. 'We want something with blood and guts and heads getting chopped off and things.'

'Sounds good to me,' I agreed.

Gemma jumped into the argument. 'We are not going to a war film and that's final.'

We finally compromised. We would all go to some film about a serial killer in a hospital. Blood and guts for us, and slush for the girls because the serial killer kissed all his victims first.

'I'll hide my eyes at the scary bits,' Leanne said dramatically.

'We'll hide our eyes at the kissing bits.'

We were all laughing so much that we almost missed Lynn wiggling past us.

She hadn't been back to the centre since that night when I had first seen Donny. So we hadn't had a chance to talk to her.

Kirsty called out to her. 'Hey, Lynn, how come we've not seen you at the centre?'

She swung round, caught sight of me and her face fell.

Mad boy in the wheelchair, still hanging around causing trouble.

She shrugged. 'Got better things to do, haven't I?' She glanced at me in disgust. 'Heard about you. You're lucky you got back. Donny's too nice, so he is.'

'We all make mistakes,' I said.

'Course you made a mistake!' she snapped at me. 'I've told you again and again that Sam went off in the van by himself. Don't you believe me, or something?'

I shrugged. 'He might have gone off and met somebody else after he left you. You don't know what he did.'

Lynn shook her head and her blonde hair rippled like a wave. 'S'pose I don't.' She looked thoughtful. Didn't say anything for a time. 'Actually, maybe I should have told you before, but I think he did go back and get Eric.'

Kirsty jumped at that. 'What did I tell you, Jamesie?'

'I tried to stop him, but he said he was going back for Eric no matter what. They were going to meet somebody else.'

'Who was the somebody else?' I wanted to know.

Lynn almost spat the words into my face. 'Somebody even worse than Eric Bethel, right?'

'So why didn't you tell the police that?' I asked her.

She sneered at me. 'Because I'm scared of Eric Bethel, that's why. And so should you be.'

'If you won't go to the police, I will.'

Lynn looked horrified. 'I'll tell them I never said it. I'm only telling you two so maybe you'll shut up about the whole thing. Do you know what Eric Bethel would do to me if he thought I'd said anything? Do you know what he'd do to you?'

Kirsty turned to me, her face white. 'That's right, I wouldn't put anything past Eric Bethel.'

Lynn looked at me as if she hated me. 'Why can't you just leave things be?'

I watched her as she hurried off.

'I knew it,' Kirsty said. 'Sam went back to pick up Eric Bethel and he met up with this other guy first, and he was the one who was driving. That's got to be it, Jamesie.'

I didn't answer her because another thought had come into my head. A really scary thought. Maybe the 'somebody worse' that Sam and Eric had been going to see had been Donny Scanlon. Hadn't I thought only days ago that his Mr Wonderful image would be a great cover-up? Maybe Eric Bethel had been cast as the villain, and the real villain behind it all had always been Mr Clean, Donny Scanlon.

But how on earth was I ever going to prove it?

My mother's life had changed too over the past couple of weeks. She had started helping out at the centre, though she let me go on a Friday night alone with my friends. And for the first time in a long while, she was making plans for the future.

'You're going back to school,' she said, just a few days later. 'We've got an appointment with Mr Simpson, the headmaster. They're going to have some adaptations made for you. They're going to make the whole school wheelchair accessible.'

'Just for me?'

'It would seem so.'

She waited, expecting me to object, and she was surprised when I didn't. But I'd known it was coming. It was the next step, after all.

Suddenly, she was crying. 'Oh, James, I am so glad things are changing for you. I'm sure it's all due to this youth centre.'

I shook my head. 'No, Mum, I know you hate to admit it, but it's due to Kirsty.'

She'd never agree to that one. Still didn't trust her. 'I don't like little girls who can lie like that,' she said.

But without Kirsty I would never have gone to the youth centre, would never have got back with Paul and Ash. Never have found my life again.

Now only one thing remained. To find out the truth about Donny Scanlon.

Chapter 22

The following Friday we all waited impatiently at the house for Kirsty. Mr Blackett had sounded the horn at least twice for us to come out to the van.

'Phone her,' I said to Gemma. 'We'll have to go without her if she doesn't hurry up.'

'I have already. She's not coming, James' she said. 'Her dad's not in yet. She won't go out until she knows he's in, safe and sound.'

I grabbed the mobile from her. 'Here, I'll call her.'

Kirsty snatched the phone up at the first ring. As if she'd been waiting beside it. But from the disappointment in her voice she had hoped it was someone else who was calling. Not me. Her dad.

'We're all heading off. The van's waiting. Are you coming or aren't you?'

Leanne let out a sigh and made a face at me. A face that said, 'Of course she's not coming, stupid.'

'I don't feel like it tonight,' Kirsty said.

'Your dad'll be all right. He's always all right. You can't wait in for him.'

Her voice became angry. 'This has got nothing to do with my dad.' There was a pause. 'Anyway, he's in already. He's making my tea.'

'Kirsty. You're living your life around your dad, worrying about him, looking after him.'

'So? He's my father. He needs me.'

Kirsty had snapped me out of my self-pity, now it was my turn to help her. 'Kirsty, you're doing the same for him that my mum was doing for me. Remember? Mollycoddling me, giving in to me. Giving up her life to look after me. You were really angry at me for letting her do that. Now I'm really angry at you because you're doing the same thing.'

She yelped. 'Oh! Jamesie's a doctor now!'

'You know I'm right.'

'You think you're right about everything. Well, just leave me be. I'll come to the centre when I'm good and ready. OK, Dad?' she called out to an imaginary father. 'Got to go, that's Dad. He's got my tea ready and then we're going to watch a video!'

The receiver was slammed down and I sat with the phone still in my hand. If only I knew how to help Kirsty. If only I could help her the way she had helped me.

Ash came back in. 'C'mon, James, the van's waiting. Are you coming?'

'Yeah, of course I am.'

Kirsty sat by the phone for a long time. She could picture James and her friends laughing on the way to the centre, making plans about going to the precinct tomorrow. James was right. She was mollycoddling her dad, but he was her *father*. She loved him. He wasn't an ordinary drunk. He had his reasons for being the way he was. Her mum dying, and then Sam.

Maybe she could go. He would be all right. Wasn't he always? He'd be in soon and he'd just go to sleep on the couch.

But what if he didn't? What if he came in and decided to make himself some chips? He'd put on the pan and then he'd fall asleep on the couch and the fat would catch fire and the house would . . . oh no! She couldn't risk that.

She sat back on the sofa and switched on the television.

He'd be in soon, she thought again.

Chapter 23

Kirsty wasn't coming. Here it was, almost the end of the night, and she hadn't appeared. So much for my pep talk.

'Gemma and me are going to go over to Kirsty's,' Leanne said. 'We want to make sure she's all right.'

Paul looked up from playing pool. 'We'll come with you, won't we Ash?'

'I'll stay with James,' Ash said, potting another ball.

I threw a bit of chalk at him. 'I don't need you here. You go and look after the girls. Just in case they get mugged on the way.'

Leanne and Gemma thought that was funny. 'We'd get better protection from cardboard cutouts.'

'Isn't that what they are?' Leanne yelped, and Ash chased her out of the door.

Paul and Gemma held back. 'We'll bring Kirsty back here, eh? We could all go home in the van with you.'

People were beginning to drift out of the centre after my friends left. I began to brush up the floor, while Mr Blackett stacked chairs and tidied up the disco equipment with the help of Peter. This had been his first night as DJ, and he had been right about one thing. He was rubbish! The music he played was absolutely awful. He was heckled and shouted at. At first I thought he was going to roll from the stage in tears. But he surprised us all. Instead of being embarrassed, he had just shouted right back and insulted everyone, left, right and centre. But his insults were so funny he had everyone laughing. Finally he had thrown a bunch of his CDs into the crowd and almost caused a fight. Luckily Anne was off for a wedding rehearsal or she would have gone spare. However, everyone else agreed it was one of the best nights we'd ever had at the disco and Peter had to promise to do it again next week.

I was in a dark corner of the disco, almost hidden from view, when I saw Lynn Mitchell sneak in.

Yes. Sneak. It was the only way to describe the furtive way she hovered at the door, her eyes darting around. Looking for what? For me?

I slid quietly back into the shadows and watched her. She tiptoed towards the office and I could see her hesitate at the door. She pushed it slightly open. 'Donny, are you there?' she said softly. Then she glanced around again before she stepped inside.

What was going on? Still pretending I was brushing up, I moved closer to the office. She had closed the door behind her, but it wasn't too hard to pick up the murmur of voices inside. Donny and Lynn. At first they could have been whispering about anything. Then, suddenly, Donny's voice was raised enough for me to hear.

'What the hell did you say that for?'

I froze. He sounded angry.

'Because it might stop the little pest thinking it was you,' she said.

'It doesn't matter what he thinks, Lynn. He can't prove anything. And I'll be away in a couple of weeks and I'll be safe. Don't you see that? You should have just let it be.'

Lynn spoke like a bad-tempered little girl. 'I was only trying to help.'

'I know but, Lynn, I think the boy likes me. I don't think he would say anything now.'

Lynn sneered at that. 'James Gordon? He's a devious little so-and-so. I wouldn't trust him an inch. I know I shouldn't say that about somebody in a wheelchair, but he is. He came back here to get you and you know it.'

Maybe Lynn wasn't as dumb as people thought. When she spoke again she sounded as if she was trying to get round him. She tried a weak little laugh. 'Eric Bethel was raging when I told him James was blaming him. He's telling everybody he's going to get him.'

That really rocked me. As if I didn't have enough problems, now I had Eric Bethel to worry about.

'Eric Bethel can be dangerous when he's raging. Lynn, what have you done?'

Lynn was obviously growing worried at Donny's tone.

'Well, that was the idea, Donny. It'll take James Gordon's mind off you if he's got Eric Bethel after him.' She seemed to think that was logical. 'And you only need another couple of weeks and then you'll be away and he can't touch you.'

Donny's soft voice was a tired sigh. 'I told you not to come here, Lynn.'

Lynn sounded petulant. 'Don't come here. Don't phone you. How am I supposed to get in touch with you to tell you anything? Sometimes I think you don't want to see me any more.' She didn't want an answer to that one. 'You're still going to send for me, Donny? It'll be brilliant in America. You and me.'

'Yes, you and me.'

Dumb as she was, even Lynn realised that Donny didn't sound too enthusiastic about that prospect.

'You better send for me, Donny.' Her voice sounded different now. Angry and threatening. 'Or else,' she said.

There was a pause. I could picture Donny looking at her, staring at her. 'Or else what, Lynn?' he asked, and there was ice in his voice.

'I just mean . . . I've been covering up for you all this time. But if you don't send for me . . . I might have to say something about exactly who was driving . . . backing up James Gordon's story.'

There was another long pause and when Donny spoke again I could almost see him smiling. 'Of course I'm going to send for you, Lynn.'

She didn't answer that and I wondered if they could be kissing. When I heard her moving closer to the door, I whizzed as far away as I could. I couldn't let either of them know that I had heard anything. I was sweating with nerves when she came out and glanced around. She had a superior little smile on her face as if she'd got the reassurance she wanted. She didn't see me. She just turned and wiggled out of the hall.

I pressed myself into the shadows, still trying to sort everything out in my head. All this time we had thought she was scared of Eric Bethel. Instead, she had been protecting Donny Scanlon. Donny *had* been driving that night, and Lynn knew it. What had Donny promised her if she kept her mouth shut? A life with him in America, obviously. And Donny didn't seem too happy about that. Lynn was beautiful but, after what I had just heard, she was as devious as she thought I was.

But if I could convince her that Donny had no intention of sending for her, and I didn't think that would be too difficult, she'd tell the truth. I bet she would. Would I sink so low? Yes, I would. Maybe she was right. I was devious. But I had found the weakest link. At last I had someone who could prove Donny Scanlon *was* responsible.

I couldn't wait to tell Kirsty. My mobile phone was in my pocket but I didn't dare use it here. Someone might hear me, and that someone could be Donny Scanlon himself.

Just then he came out of the office. He looked up and down the hall and was startled to find me there, still brushing up, trying my best to look casual. His face paled and he blinked nervously. I grinned, tried to look innocent, as if I hadn't heard a thing. Because if he realised I had, there was no telling what he would do.

However, I couldn't stop my voice from shaking. 'Hi, Donny. Good night tonight, eh?'

Donny nodded. Was he trying to look casual too? He threw the van's keys in the air, and called out to Peter. 'I'm taking Peter home,' he told me. 'Do you want to come now, or will I come back for you?'

Thank goodness. He was driving the van tonight and not Mr Blackett.

'No, the gang are coming back for me. I'll wait for them. Get things tidied up here.'

Alone, I could at least phone Kirsty and tell her what I had just found out.

Donny smiled. 'Good lad. Mr Blackett'll be somewhere about if you need him.'

It was eerie being in the centre alone. I hadn't realised just how eerie. The hall was normally buzzing but, after Donny had gone, the last few people left, one by one, calling out to me, waving their goodbyes, until there was no one there but me. Mr Blackett must have gone outside somewhere, locking up I presumed. I wheeled myself to the door and pushed it open. It was pouring with rain and bitterly cold. I stretched my neck to look along the road, but there was no sign of him or my friends yet. I backed into the main hall and decided it was safe to call Kirsty now. I was dying to tell her what I'd heard.

And that was when the lights went out.

Chapter 24

It was much later when he came in, bumping into the furniture and almost falling down in the hall. Too late for her to go to the centre now. Kirsty ran to help him and he smiled at her. 'That's my girl,' he mumbled.

She supported him to the sofa and as soon as he lay down, his eyes closed. Kirsty shook him back to consciousness. 'Dad, you need something to eat. I've got food in the oven for you.'

He waved her away impatiently. 'I'll get you some water,' Kirsty said. Mrs Thompson next door had once told her that water was the best cure for drink, and not coffee, so now it was always water she offered him.

She hurried into the kitchen and filled up a pint glass with cold water, then came back into the living-room and pulled him upright. 'Now drink this,' she ordered, sounding just the way she always sounded when she annoyed James, like a much older woman.

Her dad opened his eyes blearily, focused on the glass, waved it away. Kirsty was determined. 'Drink this down you.'

'Leave me be,' he said.

But Kirsty wasn't going to let it go. If he drank this, and more, he might not have such a headache in the morning. 'I said, drink!'

Her dad's teeth clenched. He almost spat out the words to her. 'Get that out of my face,' he yelled, and then he swore at her. He actually swore at her. Something he had never done before.

Kirsty jumped back. The water spilled on the carpet. She looked at her dad, lying there, his hair ruffled, his jaw slack. She hated drunk men. At that moment she hated her dad. She wanted to be at the youth centre tonight, with her friends. Instead, she was here with him. Looking after him, feeling sorry for him.

Jamesie was right. That was all she did. Feel sorry for him. The very thing she would never do for Jamesie.

Her dad opened his eyes for a moment. He was still a young man. Still quite good-looking. The handsomest man in the world, she had always thought. But not for long. The drink would ruin him, like Mrs Thompson's man. He'd end up with no teeth and a face with lines like a road map. The drink would make him stupid too, like the men who stood down by the betting shop, whose eyes never focused and who could never quite stand without staggering. Kirsty shivered. She hated drink.

He must have seen the disgusted look on her face. 'Did I say a bad thing to you, darlin'?' He tried to sit up. 'I'm sorry, sweetheart. Dad's had a bit too much to drink tonight. I'll feel better in the morning.'

He started to lie back down, but she pulled him up again. 'That's what you always say. But you never feel better, and the next night you have a bit too much to drink again. I'm sick of it.'

Kirsty never shouted at him. He looked startled. 'You don't have to worry about me. I'll be fine.'

'I know you'll be fine. As long as you can have your drink. You don't care about anything else.'

He began to wave his hand at her. 'Don't say that, Kirsty. It's because I care too much. I try to forget.'

Kirsty shouted right into his face. 'Well, you don't care about me, that's for sure.'

It seemed she was sobering him up better than any amount of water. 'What? I don't care? I'm your dad. Of course I care.'

'You don't know where I go. You don't know who I go with. Maybe I'm going the same way our Sam went.'

He was shaking his head, trying to blot out her words. 'No, not you. Not my little sweetheart.'

'You know who I go with, Dad? I go with the boy that was crippled in that crash. Remember he phoned here, Dad? No, you wouldn't remember. You're always too drunk. But you know what? He says our Sam wasn't driving that night. Somebody else was driving. James is in a wheelchair, and he's trying to prove our Sam wasn't driving.'

She'd got through to him at last. 'What about our Sam?' He was blinking, trying hard to sober up fast.

'He wasn't driving that night.' She screamed out the next words. 'And James knows who was driving. He'd hoped you might help him, but no, you're too drunk all the time. Somebody else let our Sam take the blame, Dad. Eric Bethel.'

That was the truth she wanted to believe, and the name made her dad straighten up. 'Eric Bethel,' he repeated. 'I never wanted to hear that name again.'

Her dad was rocking himself on the sofa, back and forth, staring at her. He said nothing for a while. 'Was that the boy that phoned here? James? He saw somebody else driving? Is that what you're saying?'

'Yeah, Dad. I'm sorry, Dad,' she said. 'He's at the youth centre now, waiting for me. And I never went 'cause I worry too much about you.'

Her dad was nodding. He looked at the glass of water and took it from her. 'Get me another,' he said. And when she came back with another pint tumbler, the first had been gulped down. He grabbed the second and downed it in one.

'Are you all right, Dad?'

'I'm fine.' He stood up. Shakily at first, and then steadier than she had seen him in a long time. 'I'm fine.'

'You're not going out again?' She was alarmed as he moved towards the front door.

'Not for a drink. I promise. I just need some air.'

He bustled out of the door and she couldn't stop him. Bumping into Gemma and Leanne on the way. Hardly noticing Ash and Paul behind them.

'Is your dad all right, Kirsty?' Gemma looked shocked as he pushed past her, heading for the lift.

'I don't know. I told him about James. I shouted and shouted at him.'

'Good. It's about time.' Leanne put her arms round Kirsty.

'He's probably just gone to get more drink,' Gemma said.

'You're a great comfort, Gemma,' Ash told her.

Kirsty shuddered. 'I hope he's not going for Eric Bethel. I shouldn't have said it was him. Why do I always tell such lies?'

That thought scared Leanne and Gemma too. 'You don't really think he'd do anything to Eric Bethel, do you?'

'I'm more frightened about what Eric Bethel would do to my dad.' Kirsty pulled at them. 'Oh come on, we'd better go after him. I've got to stop him.'

Neither of the girls could hold her back. Kirsty grabbed her coat and ran from the house.

Chapter 25

I gasped. Looked quickly around the darkened room. I could hear the rain battering against the tall windows, see some light from the street lamps outside, but inside it was black as death.

Had Mr Blackett switched off the lights, thinking everyone had gone? I hoped he wouldn't lock up with me still inside.

'Mr Blackett?' I called. 'It's James. I'm still here.'

I heard a sound. I was sure I could see a movement, somewhere near the door. Then, a voice; a voice that chilled me.

'I know you're still here.'

It was Donny.

His dark figure moved to the wall and switched on one dismal light above the battered pool table.

Donny was breathing hard and watching me. My breath caught as I saw that he had a baseball bat clutched in his fist.

'You back already?' My voice was shaking. I couldn't help it.

'I never went, James. I asked Mr Blackett to take Peter home, and not to hurry back.'

'Wha-what did you do that for, Donny?'

It was as if it pained him to answer. 'You heard, didn't you?' he said.

I tried to bluff it. 'Heard what?'

'Oh, come on, James. It's just you and me here. We can tell the truth. You heard Lynn.' He shook his head. 'Stupid Lynn. I told her not to come here.'

My voice was wavering. 'I don't know what you mean.'

He let out a long sigh. 'Oh, you know exactly what I mean, James, and you won't let it go now, will you? You're going to try to get it out of Lynn. And, eventually, I'm afraid you will.'

He sounded close to tears. 'James, why have you put me in this position?' Donny said it as if I'd done something wrong. As if all this was my fault. 'If only you could just let me get on with my life.'

'I will. I will,' I said. At that moment, I meant it. I would have promised anything. I was moving stealthily backwards, away from him.

He stepped towards me and I couldn't take my eyes off the bat in his hand. 'No, you won't.'

Now I couldn't go back any further. I was tight between the pool tables with only the wall behind me.

And still he came closer. 'When you first came back to the centre, I thought if you saw how hard I worked, you'd forgive me. Forget, think you'd made a mistake. But you never did, did you?'

He couldn't possibly mean to harm me. Surely he could never do that?

'You're not going to hurt me, Donny?'

He was shaking his head. 'I've not got any choice, James. I'm sorry. I'm so sorry.'

I was done for! But even if I was, I was going to find out the truth about everything. 'You're the one they were going to see, weren't you? Sam and Eric Bethel. You're the real baddie in all this, aren't you? The youth centre's just a cover for you.'

Even in the gloom I could see the shock on his face. His voice was trembling with anger. 'Is that what you think? Me?' He even laughed. But it was a mad kind of laughter – scary. He suddenly lifted the baseball bat and whammed it into two of the computer screens. That scared me more than anything else. He was out of control.

'That's a good one.' He was getting closer to me. Too, too close. 'That's why I drove the van that night. To *stop* him meeting up with Eric Bethel. Do you know that? Eric was taking him to meet this other guy, a real bad guy. The worst kind. Sam was desperate to go. He wanted in with the "big boys", as he called them. Ha! If he got in with them, he would never get out . . . I kept telling him that. Said he didn't care. He would make loads of dosh, that's what he said. Loads of dosh. And you know what, James?' He waited for an answer, but I knew he didn't really want one. He wanted to tell me all this. He needed to tell me.

Donny sighed and carried on. 'I stopped him. I was trying to do that stupid Sam Shearer a favour. That night, I drove because he was too drunk to drive. And because, if I hadn't, he was going to get himself into more trouble. I wanted to help him. I only ever wanted to help him. I thought, I'll take him home. Keep him away from Eric. For that night at least. But it was such a terrible night. It was the rain . . . I skidded. It wasn't my fault.'

His voice was soft, but it seemed he was screaming.

'I walked away, not a scratch. There was nobody about. The van had been thrown to the other side of the road. I couldn't see any movement in your car. Nobody saw me. Nobody knew I was there. And I thought, this is a message. A message to give me a second chance. Can you not see it was a sign, James? Why should I take the blame? Tell me why, James. I had so much to look forward to. I had just applied for this new job. In America. My whole life was opening up for me. Only Lynn knew I'd been driving and I told her I would send for her when I got to America. If she promised not to say a word.'

Suddenly he was too close. I drew in my breath. I could see those wild eyes of his. As wild as they'd been on the night of the crash.

'And then you came . . . and you remembered. And that first night when I met you here, I thought my life was over.' There was a flicker of a smile on his face. 'But not a soul believed you, did they?'

'Let me go, Donny,' I said softly. 'I'll not say a word. I promise.'

He stood up and swung the bat slowly in front of him. 'I wish I could believe it. You don't know how much I wish I could believe it. That I could just walk away and know you would forget, and let me go to America. But you won't. You're making me do this, James. Because you've got to have your revenge, haven't you?'

And even as he said that, in the middle of all my fear, I knew he was wrong. I *had* wanted revenge. All those weeks I spent in hospital, and the weeks since I first saw him, I wanted revenge. I wanted someone to suffer the way I was suffering. But not any more. My life was so different now.

I still wanted the truth. But not at this price.

'I don't want revenge any more, Donny. I thought I wanted to die, but I know now I want to live more than anything.'

'You should have died the last time. Then I wouldn't have all this trouble.'

I was breathing so hard my chest hurt. 'What are you going to do?'

'See, James, this is like another second chance for me.' He said it as if it was the most logical thing in the world. 'Eric Bethel's telling everybody he's going to get you. He'll get the blame. He's smashed up the whole place, look.' And with that he brought the bat down again against the pinball machine. 'He's the bad guy here. He's ruined his life like he's ruined so many others. And nothing ever happens to him. But me . . . one bad thing, James. One mistake. I've not got to pay for that with the rest of my life, surely?'

110

Now I was panicking. 'You're not going to hurt me, Donny! You're not that kind of person.'

' . . . I came in and tried to save you from Eric. I can't see any other way. You must see that, James. You must. I've got to do this because I'll lose everything if they find out it was me driving that night.'

Maybe I could convince him with promises that I would never tell. Maybe I could stop him hurting me by appealing to the good side of him. And there was so much good. Even in the middle of all this, I knew that. But I couldn't take that risk. My life was too precious.

I still had my mobile phone in my shaking hand and, with all the strength I had, I hurled it into his face. He was caught totally by surprise. He almost fell back, but steadied himself in an instant. In that same instant I snatched up one of the pool balls and sent it at full speed straight for him. That was a direct hit too. He yelled and this time he went down. Still, I didn't stop. I had to escape and I had seen too many horror movies where the villain looks as if he's unconscious then grabs the hero as he tries to get past him. Not this time. I was about to throw another ball when suddenly he was up with a roar, and rushing for me.

If he pulled me out of my chair, I would be vulnerable and helpless.

No! I had to move. I swirled round. He clutched at my hair, so I grabbed his hand and bit hard, right into his wrist. He was yelling, but he just wouldn't let go. And he still had the bat in his other hand. I saw him raise it, ready to bring it down.

Chapter 26

And suddenly I wasn't alone any more. Someone came rushing into the hall and Donny was hauled from me. I collapsed back in the chair as Donny staggered to his feet and stared in growing realisation at the other man.

I didn't recognise him, but Donny did. And the shock of seeing who he was made him drop the bat from his hands.

'Mr . . . Shearer . . .' His voice was desperate.

How much Kirsty's dad had heard I didn't know, but it must have been enough for him to have learned the truth. He stood for a moment looking at Donny as if he was dirt, then suddenly he ran at him again and brought him down. Rained blows into him so hard I thought he was never going to stop. Shouting and calling him the worst of names. And Donny Scanlon sank to the floor, crying, and took it all, sitting with his knees drawn up and his arms clasped over his head.

I wheeled forward. 'Leave him be, Mr Shearer. Please.' And I pulled him away.

Minutes later, Kirsty, Gemma, Leanne, Paul and Ash all came rushing into the hall. Kirsty's dad looked up at her and said softly, 'Call the police, sweetheart.'

She couldn't take it in at first. I watched her startled eyes look all around us – at her dad, at Donny and at me. Then, by the way her face crumpled, I saw that she had at last figured out the truth.

'Donny?' She still couldn't believe it. Wanted so much for it not to be true.

He didn't look up at her. He just closed his arms around his head even tighter and I heard him sob.

Kirsty looked at me now. She was trying not to cry. 'Are you OK, Jamesie?'

I was still shaking, but I smiled an answer. I was OK now. I was always going to be OK.

Ash and Paul came running up to me. 'You certainly are OK, boyo!' Ash hugged me. He actually hugged me. Then he stepped back quickly, embarrassed. 'But I mean, Jamesie, nobody's ever going to feel sorry for you again.'

We all sat in the office long after the police had taken Donny away to make a statement. The Reverend Anne had been sent for and she listened, white-faced, as she was told about Donny Scanlon. The police car turning up on the estate, heading for the youth centre, had drawn a small crowd, and Lynn Mitchell had soon returned, screaming like a drama queen. She was all tears. Clinging to Donny, she refused to leave him. 'I'll never desert you,' she had said, wrapping her arms around him as the police led him away. That thought didn't seem to cheer Donny Scanlon up at all.

'To think I used to fancy her,' I muttered to Kirsty.

'I'm glad you've seen through her at last,' she said.

'A wimp,' I said, and who would fancy a wimp?

My mum had wanted me to go to the hospital, convinced I had been hurt and was refusing to admit it. I *was* shaking, and my heart was thumping, but I was alive, and I'd never felt so grateful for it. It took ages to reassure her, but she insisted that I stay in the office drinking tea with Kirsty while she and Anne and Kirsty's dad all went back into the hall to try to clean up the mess Donny had made.

'It's going to take a bulldozer to clean that up,' Kirsty said. There was a little sob in her voice.

'Does it hurt so much about Donny?' I asked her.

She only nodded an answer. 'He was never away from the house, Jamesie, when Sam got killed. He was always there for me and my dad. How could he do that?'

'Guilt,' I said. 'And, to be honest, he was trying to help Sam that night. Keep him out of trouble. And it all went so wrong. I can understand why he walked away, let your brother take the blame. Maybe I would have done the same.'

She screwed up her face. 'How can you stick up for him now? He tried to kill you.'

'I don't know. I just don't feel bitter any more.'

And I didn't. All the bitterness had gone. I felt as if someone had opened a door in a dark room and now I was going to be able to move into the sunshine.

'Well, you were right about him and I was wrong,' she said.

I shook my head. 'No, Kirsty, we were both right.' I looked at her. 'Do you think your dad will stop drinking now?'

She let out a sarcastic laugh. 'You live in a dream world, Jamesie. He says he's going to stop, but . . . I've heard that before. He drank when my mum died and he hasn't stopped since.'

'Maybe this time he will, Kirsty. You yap on to him the way you yapped on to me, and he'll stop, just to keep you quiet. Maybe now there will be a happy ending. You've always got to be an optimist.'

She grinned. 'You have a cheek on you telling me to be an optimist. You're always moaning about something.' She poked at her chest. 'I'm the one that's the optimist.' She paused and thought for a minute. 'And what do you mean? I'm a yap? Me? I hardly ever say a word.'

'And I'm a monkey's uncle,' I said.

'I can see the resemblance.'

She always had to have the last word.

Chapter 27

Just at that moment, my mum came back into the office, followed by Kirsty's dad and Anne. Mum slumped into a chair.

'Computers are ruined. Pinball machines smashed. It's going to take a lot of money to replace them.'

'Too much,' Anne said. She flopped down on a chair too. 'I think we'll have to close the place. At least for now.'

I felt guilty. It was indirectly because of me that the centre had been smashed up. 'Why don't you get everybody who comes to the centre in here to clean it up?' I looked at Kirsty. 'Gemma and Leanne would come. So would Paul and Ash. Paul would come if Gemma would.'

Kirsty stuck out her tongue at me.

'Yeah, we could get it cleaned up, but all we would have then is an empty hall,' Anne said hopelessly.

I was thinking fast. 'Why don't we have a fund-raising disco? That equipment wasn't damaged. We could have an old-time disco, invite all the parents. Sixties music and that. Peter could be the DJ. He's rubbish but he's dead funny.'

My mum's mouth opened up in shock. 'Sixties music! Old time! I beg your pardon.'

I was getting excited now. 'We could get local firms to sponsor us.' It was as if something was clicking in my brain. 'We've got a computer firm right here in this town. Maybe they would donate computers.' I looked at Mum. 'Dad's firm would sponsor us, I bet.'

She smiled. 'I bet they would.' She bit her lip. 'I'll ask them.'

Kirsty wiggled about on her chair excitedly. 'The sports shops in the precinct – they could give us sports equipment.'

'We could do even more for ourselves,' I said. 'Organise something else to raise money for the centre.'

'A mini marathon!' Kirsty's dad said it and just as suddenly he looked at me and apologised. 'Sorry, son. Maybe not.'

But I agreed with him without any embarrassment. It was a great idea. 'Yes, a marathon. Somebody's bound to sponsor a boy in a wheelchair.' I suddenly thought of the wheelchair athletes I had seen in the Olympic events. Muscled, athletic, fit, whizzing towards a finish line. 'I'll probably go faster than my mates.'

Even Anne began to get excited. 'It's a wonderful idea. We'll start tomorrow.'

My mum insisted on taking Kirsty and her dad home. We left them at the entrance to their flats and watched as Kirsty took her dad's hand and walked beside him into the building.

'She has a lot to put up with, that girl,' Mum said.

'Ah, you like her again do you?' I asked.

Mum took a moment to answer me. 'Give me time,' she said.

I felt really good that night as we drove home through the rain. It was over at last.

'My goodness, this rain is getting worse,' Mum said, flicking the windscreen wipers on to full speed.

And, suddenly, it was just like that night again. The night of the crash, and the cars were rushing towards us – headlights glaring in my face, so bright I couldn't see anything else.

I couldn't see anything else.

The drivers' faces coming towards me were a shadowed blur behind the windscreens.

I sat up straight. I couldn't have seen Donny Scanlon at the wheel that night. It would have been impossible. Lights too bright. Too much rain.

Yet I had seen him. I had been right. He *had* been driving the van, not Sam Shearer. He had admitted it.

So, I must have seen him. There was no other explanation.

I held my breath, trying to figure out the truth. How could I possibly have known? Why had I always been so sure?

And in my memory, there was my dad again, driving our car, glancing at me in the mirror seconds before the crash and saying, 'There's something I want you to remember, son.'

I had always wondered what that something was.

Remember the face of Donny Scanlon? Had that been the something?

That was nonsense. Of course, it was nonsense . . . and yet . . . what other explanation could there be?

I sank back against the seat and smiled. 'I remembered, Dad.'